3

Must Have Connections for Inner Peace

Robin Chodak

Copyright © 2020 by Robin Chodak

All rights reserved.

ISBN-13: 978-0-9987088-3-6

Library of Congress Control Number: 2020907322

No part of this publication may be reproduced, stored electronically, or transmitted in any way or form, whether physical, electronic, or otherwise without the expressed written consent of the publisher.

Published in the United States of America

Website: www.robinchodak.com

Also by Robin Chodak

Be Gentle with Me, I'm, Grieving

Moving to Excellence,
A Pathway to Transformation after Grief

Ten Grief Lessons from Golf

Loss, Grief and Beyond
The 7th Stage of Grief

Table of Contents

Dedication

Introduction

Part I: Connection to Source..........9

Chapter 1: Learn to be Silent........................30

Chapter 2: Read Something Inspirational..........39

Chapter 3: Learn to Listen and Obey...............44

Chapter 4: Know the Truth about God (source)...62

Chapter 5: Pray...67

Chapter 6: Benefits of a Connection to Source.....73

Part II: Connection to Self.........78

Chapter 7: Emotions……………………………..83

Chapter 8: Unconditional Love………………………94

Chapter 9: Mistakes and Pain……………………...101

Chapter 10: Intuition……………………………105

Chapter 11: Joy………………………………… 114

Chapter 12: Identify with Yourself…………………...119

Chapter 13: Dreams……………………………...........124

Part III: Connection to Souls………..134

Chapter 14: Like-Minded People…………………….151

Chapter 15: Social Media …………………….....156

Chapter 16: Forgive Others…………………………163

Chapter 17: Share with Others……………………......166

Chapter 18: Understanding Energy……………………..168

Afterword: ..……………………………………………172

Dedication

This book is dedicated to my beloved husband Gerry who passed away suddenly in our home on 9/28/19. I wrote it three years prior to his death and it's been sitting in my computer. Six months after his transition I decided to revisit it in the midst of my grief and the Covid-19 pandemic. The peace I search for now is written on these pages. Gerry was my biggest cheerleader, soulmate, inspiration, and the man who was meant to enter my life after my prior husband Steve's death. We created a beautiful life together and I miss him terribly. Gerry was a well-known retired urologist who took up glass blowing and painting. He left his mark on the world with his many talents and I am blessed to have his artwork in our home. I honor him with one of his paintings on the cover of this book; it symbolizes the 3 connections I reference.

Thank you Gerry for your contribution to the world and all your love and guidance to me, it is eternal and we shall meet again. ~ Robin

Introduction

Here I am writing another book in 2016, sitting in the same chair where I started my memoir in 2006 in Michiana Shores, Indiana. It's the perfect place to get the creative juices flowing. I am surrounded by nature. I have a view of Lake Michigan from my front yard and I often see deer strolling in threes feasting on my flowers. It makes sense that they appear in threes since this book is about three connections and the number three is in the title.

The power of numbers has been very significant in my life. Three is the number of good fortune. The Pythagoreans taught that the number three was the first true number. Three is the first number that forms a geometric triangle. It was considered the number of harmony, wisdom, and understanding. Three represents time in (Past, Present, Future), (Birth, Life, Death), (Beginning, Middle, End). Many rituals perform actions three times and three is considered the lucky number! Three is the number of the Divine. In Numerology, my life path number is 33. Therefore, the power of three has destined this book for success. This will be my third published book.

While I write, I am blessed to hear the birds sing and flutter through the tall spruce and evergreen trees in my yard. The serenity of the day and the absence of street lamps at night quiet my mind and allow the words to flow from my thoughts to the paper. They don't come from my logical mind; instead, they come from a higher source vibrating with love.

As I think about the fact that my memoir isn't published I no longer get upset as I once did years ago. I realize it will come to pass in the "perfect" time. I am doing what I am inspired to do and that is to write this third book for you. I also know that no thought is a new thought, yet no one can write mine in the exact form as I do. I share my personal messages of inspiration with you in this short book. I don't believe that books need to be lengthy to have a great impact, in fact, some of the most profound books are very short such as my favorites, "As a Man Thinketh" by James Allen, "The Four Agreements" by Don Miguel Ruiz, "Peace is Every Step" by Thich Nhat Hanh, and "The Game of Life and How to Play it" by Florence Scovel Shinn.

My message is about living a "fulfilled life" or a "life you love." This can only be attained by experiencing a feeling of inner peace. You may not know what your purpose is or how to begin to live a fulfilled life. You are not alone. Until my life changed its course the same was true for me.

I have written this book to share with you what I have learned.

I yearned for inner peace! I needed it to relieve my gut-wrenching pain from grief after the suicide of my husband Steve in 2005. At that time I thought I would never recover from that dreadful day that I found him dead in our basement from gunshot wounds to his head. The clock ceased to tick in that one tragic moment. Without my soulmate my desire to live vanished. My identity slipped between my fingers and I wondered if I could survive. I wanted to put to death my anguish, but thankfully my spirit knew what I really needed. It wasn't a physical death; instead, my old way of thinking and false beliefs needed to be put to death. A new way of thinking needed to emerge. A clean, blank slate was the only thing that could do it for me. I became ready and willing for change and emptied myself to make room for transformation to occur.

In this book, I will share with you three things I have learned on my quest for inner peace after living with no hope. It's not anything new; in fact, it's what gurus have taught throughout the centuries. But it continues to be said with different words and seen through different eyes. We often make it much too complicated than it really is. I present these simple, yet life-changing ideas to you from my own personal experiences. I am blessed to have discovered them in the midst of my own tragedies and from my training as a life, grief, spiritual coach, Certified NLP (neuro-linguistic programming) practitioner, Reiki practitioner, Mindfulness Meditation Teacher, and a student of metaphysics. I reflect over my life and know that each event has created my persona as it exists today, just as each event in your life has made you become YOU. You are the creator of your life and if you don't like what it is you can begin to change it.

If you don't feel that you are living a life of inner peace then examine the three must have 'S' connections that I am going to share with you. I am not talking about the S's of wine tasting, such as smell, swirl, and sip! Although that is something I could write about as well after learning about wine in my travels to many vineyards around the world. Wine tasting is an art and a science and it helps get you in tune with your senses, especially taste. What I am referring to in this book goes beyond the physical pleasures of life. Read on to discover them. May this journey shower you with love, purpose, a fulfilling life, and inner peace that lasts a lifetime.

Part I: Connection to Source

The first of the three "S" *must have connections* to attain inner peace is **source**. You may ask what is source? What I am referring to is a creator, supreme being, deity, spirit, power, ruler of the universe, energy, divinity, celestial entity, Christ light, Jesus, or God. If any of those do not resonate with you then think of something greater than yourself that does and give it a name. I prefer to use the name God, creator, or universe and I will use those words interchangeably throughout this book. Those are ones that I connect with easily and all three mean the same to me. Maybe you don't believe in source or perhaps you do but haven't thought much about it in the past; it doesn't matter. Now is the time to consider it and it's important to give it a name that resonates best with you. A name can also be a color, shape, or smell. This will create a connection between you and your source. I offer this exercise to help you.

Sit in a comfortable position with your eyes closed.

Take a slow deep breath in and hold it for five seconds, then as you release it count to five on the exhale.

Do this a few times to center yourself and clear your mind.

Now ask from within your own being to give you a name for this higher power.

Let it come naturally; don't force anything into your mind.

Wait in silence for a few minutes.

If it hasn't come to you now don't worry.

Do the exercise again at another time. I recommend you wait until you have a name for source before you continue this book.

Most of us have formed our beliefs about source or God based on various religious teachings or lack of them. Regardless of what you have been taught, it is important for you to have a personal connection with a name. Perhaps you have negative feelings about source and that is OK. You can change your beliefs and make a connection at any time. There is no reason to feel wedded to your beliefs. You do so because you have been led to believe that you can't change them or you must be loyal to them. This holds true for religious and political ones as well. Perhaps you have had an experience in your past about God that has left a bad taste in your mouth. Don't let that keep you stuck in that place. There are many moments in life to be savored. You can change the bad taste in your mouth to a delectable one at any time.

What bad tastes have been left inside of you? Is one the taste of guilt? I have heard many stories from clients and Catholic friends about how guilt constantly slaps them in the face. It's been instilled in them as children from their religious organizations. Because of their beliefs, every choice they make is derived from guilt. They do or don't do something always hoping to escape the guilt. Those choices probably aren't the best ones for them. Sadly, they are unable to see a situation clearly because guilt has been ingrained in them and clouds their thought process. They are unable to make choices for their highest and best good. But I have seen many break through the glass ceiling and no longer buy into the feelings of guilt that once ruled their life. You are probably asking: How do you wash away the guilt that has been part of you ever since you can remember? The answer is: To connect with God or source according to your inner feelings. Do not let imposed ideas taint your thinking. Begin to think of source as an energy that exists in and around all things. This means that it is IN you and it is IN every other person. Keep your mind open to new ways of thinking about a higher source. Don't allow any religious beliefs to limit your thought process. We live in a world of infinite possibilities; yet, it is our own thoughts that limit us.

You may be wondering how to connect to source. It's not a grueling process that requires a scientific or metaphysical study. The answer may mystify you because it is pure simplicity. Here's the big news: you actually need to do nothing. The reality is that you are already connected. What an awesome awakening! It is only a matter of accepting and tapping into this truth.

How do you do it? You must learn to make choices

that radiate your essence and bring you peace. Not ones that inflict negative emotions and create bad results. Have you been living the latter for some time or perhaps your entire life? If so, you're not alone. Don't be too hard on yourself. It's really not your fault because most of your beliefs have been instilled in you by the age of eight and became part of you at an unconscious level. The good news is that you can begin to change any belief if you so choose. You may have been taught to believe that you can't change. You probably have heard some old sayings such as, "once a drunk always a drunk" or "you can't teach an old dog new tricks" and many more. The truth is, you can change, and you do have a choice. It is your God-given right. You may think it isn't attainable, but it is. I know that I make it sound quite simple and that is often hard to accept as well. You may feel in need of some expansive, thoroughly tested scientific formula. But that's not what you need. You need to believe that you have the capacity to change. If I could do it with all the garbage and guilt floating around in my head after my husband's suicide, then so can you. And now I add to this, the loss of Gerry and living in the months during Covid-19.

Know this; at any time you have the ability to break free from anything in your past that is hindering you in your life. Your mind is a wonderful machine and it responds to what you put into it. The problem is that you allow too much garbage in without your awareness. It happens from sources such as the TV, social media, or from the influence of others. The ideas from these influencers go into your subconscious mind and your brain responds on autopilot. This is one reason why you and many others live a stress-filled life. One idea that you may have been fed is that your wealth and success are the end all, be all to happiness. This belief has caused you to burn yourself out trying to achieve it. You often do this unaware of what you truly want in your life. The problem is that when you don't achieve it you work even harder and burn yourself out, even more, trying to get it.

You buy into ideas presented to you through advertising or other external things. TV car commercials are a perfect example. They often show attractive, sexy women in certain types of cars. If you are a woman you might buy into the idea that all you need is that particular car to make you attractive or sexy. Or another commercial shows an SUV filled with a family driving together on vacation. It portrays the perfect family life that you desire. Or another commercial shows a man driving an import car that picks up a beautiful woman in front of a large home. This car will bring the man the upscale status he desires, so he thinks! This is the clever goal of marketing and it often works because you buy the car or the SUV or something believing it will meet your desires. The truth is that automobiles can't bring you the true happiness you seek. True happiness can only come from within. Sadly, you are often influenced by these advertisements at an unconscious level. You make the purchase, sometimes go into debt and realize you still haven't found happiness. True happiness and peace come from the connections that I write about in this book.

Do you have things in your life that weigh you down and you long to be free from them? Is it a bad marriage, a bad job, a bad relationship, a bad financial situation, or a bad health choice, etc? Everything you experience or have experienced is a result of your choices. What they have been doesn't matter. You have bought into the belief that those bad choices from your past will continue to give bad results. That's a lie; you can begin to make choices today that will create good for you.

During the early years of my life, I learned about the importance of choice. My first awakening to this understanding happened when I became pregnant at 15. If I would have made the choice at that time not to have sex, then I wouldn't have become pregnant—it was too late. After the initial shock and fear of what I was faced with wore off, I had to think about my predicament. I was faced with another choice that would create a consequence. What do I do with the baby? Fortunately, my mom was very supportive and explained the choices that were available to me. I could keep the baby and live at home with her. Or I could keep the baby and marry the father. Or I could give the baby up for adoption. Or I could abort it. Those were tough decisions for a young girl to make, but I had to do it. My mom didn't steer me in any one direction. She let me figure it out on my own and told me she would help and support me in whichever one I chose. Wow! She is an example of an amazing mom. I realized that every choice I made or didn't make created a consequence. My decision was to keep the baby and marry the father. My choice meant that I couldn't finish high school. For many years I struggled with guilt and shame because of it. I had to live with the consequences of my choice and even though it seemed unbearable at times, I discovered later all the good it produced. I am not unhappy about my choice and I have learned to live with no regrets. In fact, I went back to school and received a bachelor's degree in computer science. I feel blessed to have a beautiful, successful, and happy daughter. She made me a grandmother at a young age. They both bring me great joy! Maybe your story doesn't appear to have a happy ending. It's OK; realize that you have the power to begin to create it now.

Perhaps you have made choices that you were unhappy with or you became unhappy later in life. This is not uncommon. It's important to not beat yourself up. There is no need to go back and revisit the past in your mind. You can't go back and redo it; therefore don't let your thoughts about it consume you. It's done. What you must do now is forgive yourself and move forward. You made the best choice you could with the insight you had at the time you made it. Learn from the experience and choose wisely next time.

After 15 years of marriage, I made another choice and it was to get a divorce. It took courage and it started my search for more meaning in my life. I believe you are searching for something more too and that is the reason you picked up this book. What is it? It's a connection to source. It's a space within your soul where divine light desires to emerge. Some call it the Christ light or Holy Spirit, some call it Buddha within, and some call it Divine Mind. Whichever you name it doesn't matter. What matters is that you let it shine within your soul.

Have you lived your life trying to connect to it but don't understand what you need to do? Do you feel or know something missing, but are unable to define it? Have you tried to fill the missing piece or void in your life with material things? It's easy to think that a certain piece of jewelry, a car, a house, or living in a certain neighborhood will make you happy and bring you peace. It's easy to buy more and more material things to try to fill the empty space. Yet, it doesn't work. Another seemingly reasonable way to fill the void is with relationships. They're good while they last but when they fail you feel empty. The emptiness causes you to try a new relationship believing the new one will make you happy. If you can't seem to get relationships to work you may turn to food, drugs, or alcohol to fill this empty place within your soul. It doesn't matter how many relationships you've had or how much material success you have achieved, you will still feel empty and continue to search for something; that is, if you haven't made a connection to source. It's important to connect with others in healthy ways but it doesn't replace the connection to source.

Even the most intellectual person often misses the obvious. The fact is divine source already resides within you, and all it wants is for you to connect to it by becoming aware of it. The problem is that you are not taught these ideas. Nor are you taught to examine your heart and mind to seek the truth. You are inundated with opposite thoughts. You are taught how to make more money, how to get a better job, how to find the perfect mate, how to have the perfect body, and how to achieve anything you want in this life. And the list goes on and on. Those things are not bad in themselves. You need many of them to live a satisfying life, but if you don't connect with your source then there will always be a gap in your soul and the empty void will need to be filled. Everything that the media feeds into your mind is about the external. If you buy into those ideas eventually you will realize that your current life is not fulfilling you. This can lead to anxiety, loneliness, sadness, depression, low self-esteem, etc.

Many people want to have a source connection but don't believe they are worthy of it. That is another false belief. Where have those ideas come from? They could have come from your parents, relatives, teachers, religious authorities, or any other person of influence. It's a lie that has been imprinted on your brain. Connection is available to each and every one of us. You are no different than me or anyone else. We all come from different backgrounds and have had different experiences and source passes no judgment on any of us.

You may be reading this and have never had any thoughts about spirituality until now. Perhaps an atheist, agnostic, or someone who didn't instill any spiritual concepts raised you. Yet, something inside is nudging you to explore deeper truths. Don't ignore them.

I wasn't raised in a very religious home, but occasionally my mom made sure her children attended the Presbyterian Church. That is when ideas began to flutter around in my head about God but they were mostly negative. I believed that if I didn't follow all God's rules he would send me to hell where I would burn for eternity. Wow, that was a heavy thought for a child to bear. Why do those ideas get imposed upon us? It was those that caused me to seek a deeper understanding as I tried to make sense of life. I call myself a mystic and a metaphysician. I believe, that if you seek the truth you shall find it. The truth comes from source and it is knowingness. You don't need to search for it from anyone else, it comes from within and you know it just "is." There is no need for definition or explanation. Have you ever had the experience of knowing something is true but can't give an explanation for it? You just know it is true! That is truth that comes from source. It's a feeling and a knowing about something that does not come from outside of yourself, but rather from inside.

Begin to think of yourself as part of source. You are part of the ONE that exists in the universe and you move, live, and have your being within that ONE. It is this ONE or this source that lets you know you are loved unconditionally and that all is well with your soul.

The universe is filled with unlimited love and power. You must learn how to tap into it and believe that you are worthy of it. I didn't have much self-worth as a young adult because of my childhood pregnancy, but as I grew older and experienced different tragedies, my eyes began to open to a larger view. I believe all the experiences we encounter pave the way for our evolution to higher thought. At 28, I lost my sister to cancer when she was 20 years old. At that time I didn't have a strong connection to source. I was filled with anger, questions, and disappointment toward God. I wavered in and out of faith trying to find and establish some type of connection.

It wasn't until I experienced the dark night of the soul while grieving my husband's suicide that I had my personal awakening or enlightenment. Thankfully, some have found it without a tragic experience in their life. During my darkest night of grief, I finally relinquished my own control and asked for the truth to ease my pain. I yearned for answers and understanding as to why I had to go through such agony. Why did my husband Steve suffer and why did I have to find him dead on our basement floor from self-inflicted gunshot wounds to his head? The anguish caused me deep despair and I no longer had a zest for living. Nothing seemed to matter and nothing made sense. Everything was incomprehensible to me. What made it more confusing was that my husband Steve was a man of faith. He lived his life with an awareness and dependence on God.

Steve was the person who brought me to a deeper faith when I married him and we attended a non-denominational church regularly. It was during those 10 years that I absorbed its many teachings. I read the old and new Testaments from cover to cover several times. I often heard scripture quoted erroneously, such as, "money is the root of all evil." That is a perfect example of how easily our minds absorb ideas, both bad and good. It actually reads, "The love of money is the root of all evil." I, along with many others have interpreted it incorrectly because of how it was told to us. That teaching was ingrained in my brain and for that reason, I made sure I didn't have too much money. The thought occurred at the unconscious level just as most other thoughts. Thankfully, I no longer believe it and any thoughts of lack are nonexistent for me. I accept that I have a right to live an abundant life, therefore I do. Money is not evil or to be feared. It has the capacity to be used for good. Steve and I had a bad break when he was diagnosed with an incurable cancer in 1999, but he remained alive after 5 years. He exhibited a desire to live. In my mind, I felt that God had given us a second chance. But when Steve died by suicide everything changed. At first, I no longer wanted a connection to God or anything else. I tried to deny any existence of a supreme being. But that didn't bring me closer to finding any sense of peace. I lived in a state of shock for several months and thought about taking my own life out of pure misery. But an internal voice began to speak to me. Whose was it? I knew it wasn't my own, because at the time mine wasn't capable of moving forward or grasping any hope. The voice was unknown to me but it encouraged me to keep going. The voice continued to speak and I discovered this was the sweet sound of spirit. It's the connection that I continually long for and one that brings me inner peace.

Chapter 1: Learn to be Silent

"Which is worth more, a crowd of thousands or your own genuine solitude? Freedom, or power over an entire nation? A little while alone in your room will prove more valuable than anything else that can ever be given you" ~Rumi

L earning to sit still with no sound blaring in your ears may seem torturous to you. Perhaps the thoughts in your brain run wild like a caged mouse all day long. You think of what you did yesterday or something long ago in your past or you think of what needs to be done tomorrow and the next day. You think, think, and think, incessantly. But are you really thinking or are you just occupying the space in your brain? For you and most people, your brain doesn't rest until you sleep. And even then, the inability to quiet your thoughts causes you to awaken throughout the night. This results in sleep deprivation, which causes the inability to function well throughout the day.

Do you spend too much time in front of electronic devices? Are you one of those people who have the TV or radio turned on to create background noise? You may not even know that you do so because it has become a habit. The problem is that it keeps from you the silence that your mind desires. Your mind is constantly filled with information. It's like a balloon ready to pop when too much air has been put into it. No wonder you feel you want to pull out your hair. It's the reason you feel overwhelmed and overworked. External media has become the thief of your private thoughts. If you want to have a connection with spirit you must learn how to clear and calm your mind. It takes sacrifice. You must say, "no" to all the demanding stimuli fighting for control of your thoughts. It's a vicious cycle until you master how to calm the churning brain. This beast must be tamed. You may think it's not possible, but it is.

There are numerous techniques that teach you how to quiet your mind. My favorites are those that I have studied and often refer to in this book. They teach you to access your senses and become aware of your thoughts. Meditation and hypnosis are other successful techniques. Many people hear the word meditation and want to run the other way because they believe they can't do it. There are many books written about it that teach specific practices. If a person tries one and fails they believe it won't work for them. The truth is no one can teach it to you. You learn it yourself. It's inherent in you and if you can breathe and let your senses become alive then you can meditate. It's really just creating peaceful moments in your reality that allows you to gain greater awareness of your spiritual nature. I have heard it described in many ways. One saying I like is: Prayer is talking to God and meditation is listening.

There are many modalities to quiet your mind and here is a simple one for you to do easily and daily. Find a place that is comfortable to sit alone and undisturbed. It means to turn off the TV, radio, iPhones, and computers. I know it sounds difficult and may sound scary for some of you, but give it a try. Ideally, sit in a room near a window to expose yourself to the outdoors. It's best to have a view of the water, trees, green grass, snow, flowers or mountains. Have at least one of those elements in your eyesight. If not, don't fret; you can still do this exercise. Simply find a picture of something in nature and place it on your window. Follow these simple steps:

1) Begin by sitting in a chair in a relaxed position. Take a deep breath in and let your shoulders feel like they drop

about 6 inches. Your shoulders are a place where you hold stress without knowing it. Once they drop you are more prone to relax. You have just given your body permission to do so. Next, feel the space between your shoulders on your back and let the blades soften.

2) Deeply breathe in through your nostrils down into your belly and breathe out through your mouth with a slight sigh sound. Do this several times with even breaths in and even breaths out until you feel a difference in how your body feels.

3) Focus on something outside your window. It doesn't matter what it is as long as it is something in nature such as a tree, bird, mountain, blade of grass, etc. Stare at it for several minutes.

4) Pay close attention to any sounds around you. It may be the whistling wind, chirping birds, distant voices, waves

crashing on the seashore, etc. Focus for several minutes only on the sound, nothing else.

5) After about three to five minutes you should feel relaxed and your mind should begin to clear. If thoughts start to invade and distract you then do the entire process again, but if distractions continue then stop and do this same exercise the next day.

It's as simple as that! You have just engaged your senses to quiet your mind. But if you found it difficult to silence your mind you can find a guided meditation. Silencing your mind is something you should strive to do each day or night for several minutes. As you do, begin to think about a creator and your existence. You will begin to feel a presence that is greater than yourself and that is when you have connected to source or God or a higher entity.

Everyone has different experiences. Some feel warmth on their body, or a sensation of being hugged, a tingling, or a presence near them. Others see light or color. Some hear voices or sounds. Whatever it is, embrace it. It is your unique experience like none you have ever had and you will know that you are connected to source or God. You will be in the presence of pure love. You will know it because you are free from any judgment or negativity about yourself and others. These are what I call moments of pure joy.

Once you learn how to access the silence you will find that you desire to be in that spiritual state more and more. It brings a sense of peace and you will notice your life beginning to change in positive ways. For example, you may not get upset as you once did over things that formerly disturbed you. Think of a time when you were driving and a car cut you off. Was your initial reaction to get mad at the driver and spew profanities loudly at him or her from your car? Maybe you called him or her an "idiot." You and many others have done it and still do. Isn't it funny that you do this when the driver can't hear you? The person has already taken off and probably doesn't know they did it. Think about this—could it be that you are really calling yourself the idiot? Why? Because you let that person get you upset and take away your power and peace. Giving your power away is idiotic, but it's often done without a conscious awareness.

Have you had another driver get upset with you? Did they yell or flip you the bird just like you do to them? If so, how did you react? Did you get angry with them for what you did? In reality, you probably didn't premeditate cutting the person off or deliberately forget your turn signal—unless you're a road warrior. What I have learned to do in those situations is something quite amusing. I first smile, then give them a wave, and then I blow them a kiss. It certainly makes me feel better and it definitely catches them off guard. They may or may not see me, but the act of a smile has already made me feel better and activated my endorphins. If they do see me I don't know what they are thinking, but I know it gives them some type of reaction. Give it a try. You will feel better too!

When you live with a sense of calm in your life then traffic and late appointments will no longer bother you. You will find that you don't take things personally as you once did. You learn to accept things as they are. The positive changes begin to flow as you make your connection with source. This happens only if you desire it, and if you do, then it shall arrive. This is called the spiritual "law of expectation." The more you expect, the more you will gain. A connection with source is never forced upon you. It's really up to you to allow it to happen.

Chapter 2: Read Something Inspirational

Reading provides you the opportunity to open your mind to new thoughts and ideas. It allows you to embrace concepts that perhaps you never knew existed. With new information, you can formulate new thinking and create a new journey for your life. Your opportunities are endless and reading opens up a whole new world for you if you so choose. Be grateful that others have had experiences before you so they could write their words of inspiration.

Reading inspirational material can help you learn and guide you to have a deeper connection to source. Read from the gurus, such as Rumi, Thich Nhat Hanh, Dalai Lama, Pope

Francis, and Eckhart Tolle to name a few. They have had their own awakening and want to share their knowledge and insight with you. Do not be closed-minded, instead be open to listening because God can speak to you through the words of others. It doesn't have to be from those I mentioned. It could be from anyone such as myself. It's easy to dismiss an idea that is foreign or goes against a belief system. Yet, it's important to keep your mind open so you can hear, see and learn from source. He may speak in the most unlikely or unexpected way.

My favorite books over the years that have altered my personal journey are; "As a Man Thinketh" by James Allen, "Science of the Mind" by Earnest Holmes, and books by Alan Watts, Sir John Templeton, Echart Tolle, Deepak Chopra, Catherine Ponder, Emily Caddy, Louise Hay, and many others. It always amazes me to mysteriously find books in my library that I don't ever remember buying.

Somehow the one that had the message I needed ended up on my shelf for me to find. I believe books are sacred. Every word and every sentence in them has energetic power that can change the course of your life. Reading allows your mind to expand beyond its limitations. You may not agree with everything written but it doesn't matter—keep reading.

Books are insights into another person's soul and are a form of communication. Have you ever read a book that profoundly touched your heart? Did you want to pass it on to someone else so they could feel the same as you? I have! I believe that books come to you and me at the time we are ready for them. This one has come to you now because there is something that you must read and absorb. Books have the power to move you from one direction to another in your life. You may have thought you wanted to go to Asia, but discovered the need to go to France! It only takes one idea from a book to change your thinking radically. Be prepared for the floodgates to open to new possibilities in your life. The words on each page are like seeds. They get planted in your subconscious and when you are ready for change those seeds begin to sprout. They grow and expand into something beautiful.

There is a slogan in Alcoholics Anonymous that says, "Take what you like, leave the rest." That idea is genius and I apply it to the books I read and to most things in my life. You may never agree completely with what someone says, writes, does, or believes, but you will connect on some level, and it's important to stay open-minded and let spirit guide your thinking. Otherwise, you will have a worldview through a narrow lens. If you want to get a broader perspective then read religious books such as the Bible and books and writings from other religions. Why wouldn't you want to challenge your mind with new thoughts? If people didn't challenge themselves to think outside the box, all things would remain the same and without accomplishments.

Chapter 3: Learn to Listen and Obey

You may still be wondering how to listen to source. I describe it as the "small voice" that is inside your heart. If you truly want to hear from God then you will learn to listen. The key is to be open and not judgmental or limited by reason. We often think that some grand encounter should define it such as the sea should part, or the sky open up, or some other profound visible sight. This isn't the case, although visible things do happen. God is both visible and invisible which means that God appears in both realms. Once we allow ourselves to quiet our minds we can begin to hear from source in any realm or form.

Have you ever had a thought that came out of nowhere? Then later you realized that the thought was the very answer to what you were seeking. That is the voice of spirit. Or, have you ever had a nudge to do something or call someone or go somewhere? But you ignored it and just kept on your merry way. Did you have a fleeting thought for a moment and then the busyness of your mind erased it? It's easy to pass those off as nothing and believe they have no spiritual validity. But is it something else? Yes! It is the voice of spirit trying to get your attention, but the problem is that you filter it out. When it comes, you don't know from where it came so you don't trust it. Or you don't want to spend time listening for the answer so you just ignore it. You must learn to no longer do that if you want to communicate with source or spirit.

I was awakened to spirit many times after the suicide of my husband Steve in 2005. One, in particular, felt like a sledgehammer to my head. Many times it's what we need—a hard knock to wake us up to spirit because we live so distant from it.

Steve was a musician and began playing in bands starting in his teenage years. I also had a love for music, therefore much of our life together revolved around it. Steve sang and also played the drums and keyboard, but the guitar was his love. In fact, he had eight of them in our basement where our recording studio was set up. We spent many hours playing music together. I usually played tambourine while I listened to Steve strum the chords to his favorite rock and roll bands. The Beatles were gods in his mind. George Harrison was his favorite Beatle and he could play every one of his songs. The walls in our home vibrated with the sounds of music. After Steve died, I didn't want to hear another musical note and certainly not the Beatles singing, "All you need is Love." On rare occasions I turned the radio on and if a Beatles song played I felt a gnawing pain and loss of breath. My heart ached and I would turn the music off immediately.

About a year after Steve died I had the radio on and a Beatles song played—instead of turning it off I felt a sense of comfort and let it finish. This happened again a few days later. The third time it happened a warm glow filled the room. As I searched the room to try to understand this phenomenon my eyes landed on the digital clock in the kitchen. In big, bright, bold numbers, it read 11:11 as plain as day. The Beatles' song seemed to play louder. I let it finish and felt soothed. I was proud of myself but didn't give it too much thought. Two days later the same thing happened. Another Beatles song came on and again the clock read 11:11. I felt the same comforting energy in the room and warm glow. I knew it was Steve's spirit letting me know that he was well.

I also sensed that everything in my life would be OK if I trusted the universe. Over the next few weeks I continued to see 11:11 or 1:11 on the clock every single day and every time there was a calming energy in the room. I could not ignore this strange recurrence and researched possible meanings. I discovered that according to numerology the number 1 is a power number. Some believe it is an angel number. It also says number 1 resonates with the vibrations and attributes of new beginnings, creation, independence, uniqueness, motivation, ambition, willpower, and positivity. Number 1 also aligns with energies of self-leadership and assertiveness, initiative, instinct and intuition, organization, achievement and success, strength and self-reliance, tenacity, forcefulness and authority, and love. It also resonates with inspiration, attainment, glory, happiness, fame, fulfillment, unity, the divine presence, will and focused consciousness, and the ability to use personal resources. The meaning was all positive and defined things that I wanted in my life; therefore I couldn't ignore its incredible awakening. It was the voice of spirit speaking to me.

Number 1 encourages us to step out of our comfort zones and reminds us that we create our own reality with our thoughts, beliefs, and actions. Wow, after I read its meaning I paid close attention to it. I believed in the power it held and wanted to experience all that it said. The numbers were calling me and they became a part of my life. Actually, they were already in it before I knew it. They had emerged before I acknowledged them, specifically when Steve and I married on 11/11 in 1995. I had no idea when I planned the date that those numbers held great significance and would become a powerful source to me. But I do not doubt that Steve connected to them and knew their purpose. In fact, his life path number is a ONE. Even though he is physically gone, every time I see those numbers there is a comforting energy present. It is not by chance that I am writing this book 11 years after my awakening to the number 1. Since that time I see it in some form every single day, sometimes numerous times a day. It's my sign that a higher power is always with me. It's also a sign that Steve's energy is near and you and I and everyone are all part of ONE entity or ONE substance.

Those numbers were in my life often without my knowing their power or profoundness of them. An example is a beautifully framed scripture verse that was given to me after Steve's cancer diagnosis. Many times the words comforted me when I was in deep despair due to watching Steve suffer the horrible side effects of his cancer treatment. I often stopped in front of the picture to read them out loud. Somehow they gave me the strength to make it one more day. They read, "For I know the plans I have for you, sayeth the Lord, They are plans for good and not for evil, to give you a future and a hope." The Old Testament scripture is Jeremiah 29:11. My mind sees 2+9 =11, therefore it reads as 11:11. It wasn't until after Steve's death that I discovered that verse in a whole new way.

Those numbers come to me when I need confirmation or guidance about a decision I must make for my life. For example, I will receive an email at 11:11 or 1:11 or with a combination of 1 and 0 to confirm an answer to something I was seeking. I have many events that support it. One occurred during the time I was searching for opportunities to get my writings published. Out of nowhere an author contacted me and wanted me to write an excerpt for his book on grief. He knew nothing about my experience with 1's. The amazing thing was that my personal survivor story ended up in chapter 11 of his book. I don't believe it was by chance. You can verify it in Tom Sweetman's book, "From Grief to Greatness."

Another example occurred when my new husband, Gerry and I were buying our condo in Florida. We bid on several but were continually outbid by someone else. Finally, I saw one, yet felt unsure, but when I noticed the address 2901 I knew it was "the one" since 2+9 =11. My mind saw it as 1101. Therefore, the uncertainty that I had about the purchase ceased and I knew that 2901 would be my home. My belief held true; we didn't get outbid. We won! Those are just a few uncanny examples. But similar situations happen to me all the time and those numbers guide me. Every time I see them, I stop, reflect, and thank God for the peace I have found in my life and the guidance I know that I will always receive. In fact, I must tell you one more story about when those numbers came into play with a very strong vibration. After Steve died in 2005 I had an inherent knowing that one day I would be married again. I didn't know when it would occur but it was my soul's desire. Again, my belief came to fruition—I remarried on 11-11-11 to a wonderful man named Gerry. After we met, I shared with him my encounters with the number 11 and interestingly he began to see them every day too! We both chose that date because we knew the mystical profound energy surrounding it. I knew there was a greater source involved in my meeting and marrying Gerry, just as I knew it with Steve. I am grateful for each of those spirit-guided moments with the number 1.

Perhaps the number one doesn't have any meaning to you and that's OK. Maybe another number is popping up to you all the time. You must begin to pay attention to them. It's one of the ways that spirit is trying to get your attention.

If you want to begin to obey the promptings of spirit you must learn how to listen. Here is an exercise to help you awaken to it. Pay attention to the next time a thought enters your mind that seems to come from out of the blue. When it does—I want you to do the following:

1) Stop whatever it is you are doing at the time. If you can't at the moment—stop as soon as you can.

2) Write the thought down on paper.

3) Write what you were doing at the time of the thought.

4) Write the time of day.

Perhaps you were driving, exercising, showering, listening to music, etc. Whatever it was write it down. Then look at your words, and say them out loud. It's important to do so. It helps keep the busyness of your mind from clouding out the words. Then hold the thought for a few minutes. Sit with the thought for as long as you can. Don't judge it. Then go about your day. In a few days refer to the thought and see if anything else in your life was connected or derived from it. Pay attention to the time and what you were doing. Many times the thought will occur while doing the same thing at the same time. Spirit wants your attention. But the problem is that your mind may not have been listening. The exercise is designed to help you create awareness when spirit is speaking. If you continue to do this you will "know" that it is spirit, or source, or God.

Have you ever had thoughts in the past to call someone or go to a certain place but you ignored it? That was the divine spirit in you! Once you become cognizant of these thoughts you will no longer ignore them, instead, you will act upon them. For example, the thought comes to you to call a friend you haven't spoken to in years. You acquiesce and learn he or she has been trying for some time to get in contact with you. The reason—they felt compelled to share some information with you. Guess what? It was the information you needed about a job, relationship, or something for which you were seeking an answer. Can you see the results that transpire when you listen? That is a simple example of how it works! The thoughts or promptings are from spirit and they are guiding you. So don't pooh-pooh them any longer. Those thoughts that once came to your mind out of the blue that you ignored are valuable and will create your highest good. You have just learned a profound secret.

    Spirit often speaks to me when I am biking. It is during that time that I quiet my mind enough to hear from God. It's when ideas or exact sentences for my writing come into my thoughts. Sometimes I can write an entire blog post in my head. I know it comes from spirit because many of the thoughts are not ones that I would be planning. I have received messages to go to specific places or call certain people that I never imagined going to or calling. When I first began the practice of listening, I struggled because my ego was in the way. I call it the ego-mind or the mind that wants to Edge God Out. It would butt in and say, why bother this person or why waste your time? Nothing good will come of it or that is an absurd idea! Fortunately, I have learned how to turn off my ego chatter. I also learned not to judge spirit's guidance because it knows what is needed for my highest good much better than I do! I have learned to no longer ignore those promptings.

In the past, if someone had popped into my head that I hadn't seen for years I typically didn't do anything with the thought. Now, if it happens I act upon it and am guided on what to do. I no longer let the thought vanish, push it out or ignore it or judge it. Every time I have acted based on the thought it has always turned out to be a positive experience for me or the other person. These occurrences happen because I meditate, pray, sit in silence, ask for guidance, and trust that spirit will bring the answer. If you want to learn to listen you must do the same. The answer will come and it's up to you to listen. You may not know at the exact moment what the result will be, but know that it is energy in motion and it will create good for you.

People always ask, how do you know the thoughts are from God and not your own? If the thought is bad you can be assured it is not from God. There is nothing that God wants for you but the best. They are thoughts that will bring something good to you and to others. It's not from God if the thoughts will harm you or someone else. Spiritual concepts are hard to describe in mere words because they are often surreal and create awe. The best way to describe it is that there will be an energy surrounding you and you will have a certain sense that what you are doing is right and good!

You are part of the human race that is created as sentient beings. This gives you the ability to sense, know and feel. Sometimes it displays as a feeling in your heart or it can be an overwhelming emotion of pure bliss. Labeling the experience often diminishes it. It's best to let it absorb into your consciousness. This is a transformative process. The more you tap into all your senses the more you will connect with yourself and with source. The more connection you have with source—the more you will be assured that your thoughts have come from source. If you leave yourself out of the equation, source takes over and a channel opens up to its magnificent power.

My connection to source didn't happen until I started to

spend time alone. That meant with only me, myself, and I and pure positive energy. I spent hours in silence as I yearned for something more than my pain. This meant no TV, no connection to social media, no interaction with other people, just me and my divine guiding power. My grief was the catalyst for my source connection. As I reflect on all the events in my life I wonder if I would be in my existing state of peace in the absence of my suffering. It is not a question that can be answered nor does it change my current existence. My life has meaning in the moment-to-moment experiences that carry me on my journey each and every day.

I am not suggesting that you need to go through intense suffering to attain a connection to source, but many have discovered it because of their own traumas and tragedies. I believe that if you desire a connection to source and to self then you shall receive one. You will take in all that you are ready and open to receiving. God never disappoints those whose souls are aligned with his design.

Chapter 4: Know the Truth about God(source)

If I ask you to think about God what comes to your mind? Is it a man? A woman? An entity? Where does God reside? Does God have a color? Does God have a personality? Does God have a shape or a size? Some of you could probably answer this question fairly quickly. Much of your ideas have been ingrained into your mind from your upbringing and those who have influenced your life. Perhaps some of you are still trying to formulate an answer as you read this.

Some of you may conjure up an image of a God who sits

on a throne in a place called heaven. His authority delivers rewards to those who obey and punishment to those who do not. That idea was closely aligned with mine at one time. But today, I no longer hold those ideas after many experiences and tragedies in my life. Steve's suicide was a pivotal turning point for me. I don't believe that an all-loving God would punish a man for taking his own life because of his mental anguish. Yet, I know there are some who do. I argued with my own beliefs. If I believed that God was good and God made man in his own image, then the conclusion was that Steve was good. In fact, he was one of the most loving, giving, kind men I have known. If God is ALL Goodness and created man from his goodness, then it is against the nature of God to punish that which he created like himself. Therefore, Steve could not be punished. My pain, my questions, and my deep search for truth brought me to a different understanding of God.

My belief is that our souls long for a connection to God or a higher source and we experience it through our heart, mind, and senses. Science determines to understand God based on the knowledge of facts and proven principles and religion through history and dogma. You must come to your own conclusions about God; no one can force them upon you. They will come when you are open and receptive to your soul's yearning.

My new thoughts about God have brought me inner peace and I share them now with you. God is truth. God is love. God is All. God is omnipresent or everywhere, omnipotent or all-powerful, and omniscient or all-knowing. God is infinite wisdom. God is spirit. God is in All people and in ALL things. God is unchangeable. God is both visible and invisible. You are never alone because God is always with you. God is the universal law. God is part of me and I am part of God, just as a wave is part of the ocean. Unity is experienced with the awareness of your Oneness with God and the Law. Opposition is removed from your consciousness regarding separation. Do you believe these things about God? If so, then you must accept that you are part of God and you have part of his character. If you believe that you are separated from God or Source or the Universe you are limited by the thought of separation. When you perceive yourself as part of God you accept that nothing is impossible for you. The problem or lack of inner peace lies within your own mind. You must begin to change your old way of thinking that is filled with limitations. Perhaps even now you are limiting God's power in your life or you are limiting your thoughts to what I am writing. You may be judging and blocking these ideas. It's OK. It's the way your mind has been programmed. The unknown often creates fear and resistance. It's important to be open and receptive and

God's truth will be revealed to you. There are many religions and they may have influenced your beliefs but there is only one higher entity in the universe. Ask for guidance and be willing to observe things from a new perspective. This will enlarge your territory and open a new world to you.

Chapter 5: Pray

If you want to have a connection to source you must engage in some form of communication, such as prayer. Without communication, intimate relationships cease to exist. Think of it in practical terms. If you don't communicate or talk with your family members you wouldn't have much of a connection with them, would you? Not really. Therefore you must spend time talking and listening to them. It creates trust and builds bonds. Talking or praying to God or your higher power is the same. I am sure you have your own ideas about prayer and how to pray. First, I will tell you what I believe prayer is not. It's not a ritual or a bunch of lengthy impressive words that you use to beg God to give you what you want. Prayer is a mighty force in the universe. You may have heard it said, prayer changes things, or the family that prays together stays together. I believe this is true. Why? Because it is the act of praying that changes you. God is not the one who needs changing because God "Is". What prayer does do is change your consciousness about yourself, about others, and about your experiences.

I believe the act of prayer transmits energetic vibrations to God, to the one who is being prayed for, and to your own spirit. Thus, the reason people testify to positive results or miraculous healings after prayer. Change occurs because your thoughts transmit energy into the universe and that energy must create. An action must be completed from its transmission. Therefore the generated results of prayer will always be the ultimate change of one's existence.

My prayers consist of love, gratitude, and blessings to others. In the past they weren't always that way; in fact, they often were sprinkled with bargaining and begging. My knuckles tightened during my grasping for words and I usually felt a pit in my stomach afterward, worried that the results depended on my execution of the task. I didn't feel very confident and was a victim of imposed beliefs about prayer. Thankfully that has changed, and I believe prayer is a gift that I can give to another person. As I pray for someone I think of them as perfect and whole. I don't think of him or her as sick or diseased. Positive, pure thoughts are what I send to them and to God as I envision them healed. You have heard stories of people miraculously healed from disease, right? Could it be from the prayers of others? Or has the person changed his consciousness and seen himself as whole or healed? Many unexplained occurrences have been reported. These miraculous healings are considered the mysterious workings of a divine entity. Science is unable to prove them, yet they exist. I believe the reason is due to "prayer."

You may be questioning if you should pray or not? The answer is yes! Why? It allows you to contribute to someone else's good. Also, it keeps you humble and keeps you in an attitude of gratitude. Every morning one of my rituals is to "TUG." It's an acronym I created that means, "Thank U God" and it daily spews from my lips. In simplistic terms, it's me talking to God. Prayer creates a connection and oneness with God. The connection elevates your senses. I experience it in many ways. One is through the ocean as my senses are heightened by it. I am awakened to the energy of it as I look upon it. Not only do I see it, but I also have the joy of feeling it when I dip my toes into the water along the shore. I also smell the crispness of the ocean as the water rushes upon me and I taste its saltiness as the droplets hit my lips. The sound of the waves crashing along the shore lulls me to sleep during the night. In those moments I become part of the ocean, just as I am part of God. I feel one with all. Prayer allows you to connect and experience this oneness with God or the universe. It's a communication with your soul and source.

You may think that it is difficult for you to pray. It can be—if you're inside your head. When you're in your head it means that you are engaging your conscious or logical mind instead of your heart. I certainly know when I am in my head because I don't feel connected and rush the process. It's not genuine. You need to let the language of your spirit speak. Try this exercise as a way to begin.

- Place your hand on your heart.

- Feel the rise and fall of your breath.

- Visualize your heart pumping and radiating love from God and through whom you are saying the prayer.

- Imagine the prayer as a light beam of energy traveling through time and space to reach the person.

- Begin to feel love, be love, and send love.

This exercise allows you to connect with your heart as you pray. The more you do it the language of spirit will begin to flow during your prayers.

I believe Mother Teresa understood the meaning of prayer when she said, "If we really want to pray, we must learn to listen; for in the silence of the heart God speaks." I couldn't agree more! Prayer is both listening with our heart and speaking using the language of spirit.

Chapter 6: Benefits of a Connection to Source

Why do you want a connection to source? I believe we are the result of a grand design that demands a connection. I like to think of it as electricity in a house. A flick of a switch turns on the lights in your home. How does it occur? It happens because there is the main source of power that is connected to the switch. The switch activates the electricity, which then causes the room to illuminate. Think of yourself as the switch and God as the power or source. It's a connection that results in something that becomes activated. Therefore when you are connected to source you activate power or good in your life.

There are benefits to having this connection. When you are

connected to source, you know that "someone is always watching your back," and that someone happens to be a higher being who can be called God. This knowledge instills a sense of inner peace within you because you know that you are protected. You no longer need to live your life in a fearful state because you will know that everything is working for your good. You no longer judge situations by how they appear. Appearances are only your perceptions anyway. I love this acronym for fear and I say it often; Fear is False Evidence Appearing Real. If you are living in fear, you are looking at a situation from your own perspective and it is often related to your former false beliefs. But in actuality, God hasn't created the situation in that fashion. God does not create fear, you do.

You may have fears about your future because the unknown is frightening to you. Do you worry constantly about many things such as; losing your job, not paying your mortgage, not finding a companion, losing someone you love, getting an illness, or fear of your own death? And the list goes on and on. Do you find yourself caught up in this fear-based attitude? Could it be a lack of the truth about God and lack of a connection? A secure connection to God allows you to release those fears and if they do arise, you can much more easily dismiss them when they occur. Connection to Source provides the assurance that situations will work to your advantage.

God has already designed your life for the ultimate good. The problem is you don't believe it and you make choices that move you away from your good. God is not a puppet master and certainly isn't somewhere yonder holding strings attached to you as if you were a marionette doll. The universe has given you and everyone free will and free choice. The benefit of being connected to source is that you will be guided to make choices for your highest good. Your choices will no longer be destructive and self-sabotaging.

Another benefit is a sense of "knowingness" that you will begin to have about certain situations in your life. Another way to say it is that, "you will just know it." You may not be able to give a dissertation on the fact that you do know, but you just do. This comes from the connection with a divine source and the assurance of guidance and protection.

Don't confuse your connection to God as your being equal to God. Equality is not possible, but similarity or "part of" is already in existence. Think of God as a big circle and in the circle is all of creation. You and everyone else are in and part of that circle and each one is necessary to sustain the circle. You are not equal to it because any part of something does not equal its whole. A better way to say it is that you are one with God, or immersed in God, or living within God. Everyone is an individualized expression of God. Can you understand that the benefits of a connection to Source will lead to your inner peace? I hope so. Begin to do the things I suggested to get you started on your journey.

Part II: Connection to Self

The second connection that you must have to find inner peace is a connection to self, meaning *yourself*. That may sound strange to you since you are yourself. But are you really connected or associated with your being? You may often live your life disassociated from your feelings or desires. This is not always a bad thing. In fact, it is necessary many times to disassociate from yourself to unravel a problem. You must step away from a particular issue and see it from another person's perspective. As you begin to get in connection or in tune with yourself then you will know when to move away from a problem.

It's important to know yourself in sensory terms. When it comes to the olfactory sense or your sense of smell most of you can easily identify with it. You know which perfume scents tantalize you and which ones don't. You know if lavender is pleasant or not. Some of you like patchouli oil or the smell of a burning fire. For many, the smell of gasoline is considered to be repulsive. There are certain herbs and spice aromas that please you. Garlic may be a smell that you love and it elicits memories of your grandma standing over the stove in her apron cooking spaghetti sauce. Most people can associate with the sense of smell unless a health issue is involved. Most of you also have a strong connection to the gustatory sense or that of taste. There are certain foods that you only need to think about for a second or two before heading toward the fridge or cabinet to satisfy your craving. Sometimes the urge is so strong that you drop everything you are doing to run out and get what you want; perhaps it's a pizza or an ice cream cone. Have you done this? I certainly have.

Your sense of taste lets you know if you like or dislike chocolate, cookies, certain vegetables, fruits and meats. Knowing your taste buds helps make shopping, cooking, and dining-out choices easy since you know what you like. You frame your life around the things that appeal to you and the more you understand what they are, the easier your life becomes.

Connecting to self will eventually lead you to a fulfilling life and a sense of inner peace. What does it mean to connect to self? It means to begin to know yourself and who you are intimately.

Have you ever boarded an airplane ready for a flight and wondered where the plane was going to take you? Of course not! You know the pilot has the flight plan and knows the destination. He knows how to fly the plane and get you to your desired location. You must realize that you are the pilot of your life and can get yourself to your desired destination!

Most people walk around in a hypnotic state in their everyday existence. They live like a robot. It starts with the alarm clock to get them to work on time and ends with falling into bed at night. Many people are constantly fatigued due to excessive work hours. If they have families, they rush home to spend time with them. They do the necessary things to keep up their homes, such as cooking, shopping, cleaning and managing the household and finances. They often need medication to help them sleep and need extreme amounts of caffeine to help them function during the day. They have no time to learn who they are and what they need. All they do is rush, rush, rush! They are living apart from themselves. Does this sound like you? If yes, don't worry; you have the capacity to change. How? First, you must acknowledge that you need to do things differently and second you must create a connection with yourself. Your inner spirit is the power that knows itself. It's the only power that is self-knowing. You start the process by knowing your emotions.

Chapter 7: Emotions

According to Dictionary.com, emotions are any strong agitation of the feelings actuated by experiencing love, hate, fear, etc., and usually accompanied by certain physiological changes, such as increased heartbeat or respiration, and often overt manifestation, like crying or shaking. Do you realize how much your emotions affect you? It is possible to learn how different experiences affect you and what emotions you feel as a result of them. For example, how do you feel during and after an argument with a friend? Do you feel anger? Does your body feel any sensations in any particular area such as throbbing or heat? Understanding your reactions is the beginning of self-discovery. Perhaps you have not been on this journey and this is the reason you find yourself unhappy much of the time. The inability to determine the cause of your emotions or feelings has left you in a stuck state. You haven't allowed any time in your life to discover your desires and what your emotions mean. Living this way can lead to depression for many people. They often turn to prescription medications or self-medicate with drugs or alcohol to get some relief.

What you must do to begin your journey of self-discovery is to learn about your emotions. You do this by first recognizing the emotion you are feeling at any given time and second by understanding what causes it. For example, if you find that you are not feeling like "yourself" then you must discover what emotion has caused it. Is it anger? If so, then what caused you to become angry? Was it because your child broke one of your household rules? Or was it because your boss ignored your recent contribution to the company and gave credit to someone else when you felt you were the one who deserved it? Or could it be a good friend who forgot your birthday? Maybe you didn't feel anger, instead, you felt hurt. It's important to know the difference. Those are some examples and you probably brush them off as nothing and go about your day in an uncomfortable state. But later you find yourself flying off the handle because your child spilled his or her milk. It wasn't the spilled milk that triggered your reaction—it was the unrelated event that happened earlier.

In reality, you often act inappropriately because you haven't addressed your underlying emotional state. Why, because you haven't paid attention to yourself and what your self needs. The first step is to identify the emotion and then take time to think about the cause. This helps you learn to get in tune with yourself. It sounds so simple, but many of you reading this aren't aware of the reasons you feel the way you do, especially when negative emotions are involved. You must understand what makes you angry, disappointed, happy or sad, etc. For example, did you feel sad when a friend didn't invite you to a party? Write it down. It's necessary to stop and study each one of your emotions separately and learn how they trigger you. If you are serious about this then your assignment is to write down next to each of the emotions what causes you to feel it and how you feel it. I want you to associate where you feel the emotion in your body. For example, do you feel anger in your chest? Does your breathing increase? Do you feel sadness in your heart? Does it beat faster? Notice the effect of the emotion on your physical body. Do your hands begin to sweat? It's important to pay attention to these feelings as well. This will help you get to know yourself or connect to yourself in a deeper way.

This is not a complete list of emotions and if you experience one not listed then be sure to add it.

First complete the negative emotions:

Emotion	Cause	Feeling in your body
Angry		
Disappointment		
Sad		
Jealous		
Insecure		
Fear		
Powerless		
Hurt		
Envious		
Guilty		

Next are some positive emotions. Do the same as above. Write what causes you to feel the emotion. For example, do you feel *joy* when you hold an infant? If I have missed any emotion you experience be sure to log it as well. This exercise will help you get into touch with your inner self and create the connection necessary for inner peace.

Emotion	Cause	Feeling in your body
Joy		
Hope		
Happy		
Courageous		
Secure		

Calm		
Powerful		
Trusting		
Grateful		
Satisfied		

It might take you a period of days, weeks, or months to get through all those emotions. Just keep at it. The next assignment is to help you begin to recognize how often you experience each of these emotions.

Below is a weekly checklist. Mark the day you are feeling the emotion. This will allow you to keep track of each one and how often you experience it.

Emotions	Mon	Tue	Wed	Thur	Fri	Sat	Sun

Angry							
Disappointed							
Sad							
Jealous							
Insecure							
Fearful							
Powerless							
Hurt							
Envious							
Guilty							
Joy							
Hope							
Happy							

Courageous							
Secure							
Calm							
Powerful							
Trusting							
Grateful							
Satisfied							

If you are diligent about these exercises you will find that you will begin to understand more about yourself and your emotions. This allows you to have power over them and you can begin to change your responses to situations that once caused you discomfort or pain.

    I discovered that I experience the emotion of joy when I ride my bicycle. My heart beats at a steady pace and a smile forms on my lips. As I pedal along with a carefree spirit I am delighted by the cloud formations. I see the many different shapes, colors, and movements of the clouds that are ever-changing in the vast blue sky. I become aware of the supreme entity that created the magnificent collage and I feel humbled to share in its beauty. At the same time, it brings me a sense of gratitude. I recognize how fortunate I am to be healthy and able to ride my bike. Sadly, many people don't have the ability to do so. When I am in this state it ignites more gratitude and I begin to think of the many things in my life that make me thankful. The experience of cycling gives me extreme pleasure. After I finish my gratitude list, my mind quiets and I allow spirit to fill my thoughts. It's during these times that I receive insights and messages from God. Each bike ride is a new joyous experience for me. Most of my writing has been dictated to me during my rides. It's important for you to find a time when you can quiet your mind to hear from God. It may be a physical activity. Or perhaps it's listening to music, playing an instrument, painting, or another art form. Whatever it is, it's important to get in tune with it. These activities will help you know yourself at a deeper level and not feel disassociated from source.

Chapter 8: Unconditional Love

To have inner peace you must learn to love yourself unconditionally. For many of you, it may seem impossible since you don't even like yourself. Do you look in the mirror and think negative things about yourself? Do you hate the way you look? Does the person who is staring back despise you? Are you disgusted for feeling the way you do about yourself? If you answer yes to any of these it's critical you begin to change the opinion of yourself.

You can do it with this simple, practical exercise. Do it every morning for 21 days and see what happens. Twenty-one days is the powerful, proven number. It's when "magic" begins to happen!

Day 1. Look into the mirror for 1 to 2 minutes. Then write down everything you thought without censoring your answers. For example, if you "hated" your hair, write that down. If you noticed "gray" write it down. If you noticed wrinkles, write it down. If you felt "sad" write it down. If you felt "angry" write it down. Write down whatever flashed through your mind in those short minutes.

Day 2. Look into the mirror but this time I want you to say, "I love myself exactly as I am." Say it five times out loud while looking directly into your eyes.

Day 3. Go to the mirror. Think of any positive things about yourself and say them out loud into the mirror.

Starting on day 4, repeat day 3. Do this for the next 21 days and you will notice a difference in how you feel in general. You will definitely feel better about yourself. You may think that these exercises seem trite and silly.

Yes, they may be, but they are powerful. Every cell in your body responds to every thought you ever think or speak. This is the mind, body connection. If you want to have a healthy body, then those are the thoughts you must think. If you constantly complain about how you feel, your body will respond to those complaints and bring on the suffering. The study of epigenetics explains how your emotions regulate your genetic expression. Researchers have demonstrated that your genes respond to your conscious thoughts, emotions, and unconscious beliefs along with environmental factors such as nutrients. Cellular biologist Bruce Lipton, Ph.D. is one of the leading authorities on the subject and explains it in his book, "The Biology of Belief."

It's important to become aware of the mind, and body connection. I certainly did. I became weak and depressed because my mind stayed stuck in a state of grief for many months. It wasn't until I understood the connection between the two that I began to change my thoughts. If you are serious about finding inner peace then do the suggested exercises. You will create a powerful connection to yourself and begin to get control over your thoughts. They will no longer run loose in your head like caged mice on a wheel. Everything anyone has ever accomplished started with a single thought! If you want success in your life you must have thoughts of "being successful." No person who has ever climbed the ladder to success thought they were a loser and couldn't succeed. They began to "think" and "see" it and then it came to "be." Warren Buffet, one of the wealthiest men in the United States understood this when he said, "I always knew I was going to be rich. I don't think I ever doubted it for a minute." We should all be thinking like Warren.

If you want inner peace you must walk the path to

achieve it and the three connections that I write about can lead you to it. Anything you want to accomplish must first come as a thought in your mind. For example, this book came to me as an idea one day while I was riding my bike. I could have let the thought dissipate into thin air as I pedaled along my merry way enjoying the scenery. But the thought came over and over again. I have learned not to resist. The next step was to take action. I stopped my ride and made notes on my iPhone. When I arrived home I put the words on paper. This began the process. Every day I said a prayer for spirit to guide me and I would sit in front of my computer ready to write. Some days nothing came and I accepted it. I have learned you can't force spirit. I am confident this book is divinely inspired and it will reach those who are meant to read it and accept it. It's not for the faint of heart; instead, it's for you who desire something more in your life. Money can't buy it nor can another person give it to you. It's your own inner peace.

Once an idea comes to you it is necessary to act upon it. If you want success you must keep working towards your goal. It may not happen overnight, but you must persevere. I began to "image" or "see" this book as finished and I saw it being read by many people. I envisioned it as an inspiration tool to help you on your journey to find inner peace. My thoughts brought it into manifestation. The same process can work for you. I don't have a special gene to accomplish it, nor does Warren Buffet, Steve Jobs, or Bill Gates. But what I do have in common with them is a desire for manifesting success. When you or I have the desire and the knowledge to manifest our highest good the universe does not create resistance, it only responds.

As you connect with yourself and love yourself, you exercise the universal "law of love." This love for yourself extends to family and friends and eventually the world around you. When you show love to yourself you are actually showing love to God or source because you are One with God.

When you love yourself unconditionally you should be asking, what is the good that I want to experience? You must be definite about the life you want to live. This takes serious thought, but it's important. If you know what you want, you can have it. Do you love yourself enough to do this? Can you believe you deserve it? Many of you reading this may not. But if you understand that you are God's magnificent creation you will also understand you deserve all His goodness. When you begin to love yourself as God loves you, then you will allow the good to flow into your life. Unconditional love never keeps track of wrongs and it always forgives. To forgive is the highest and most beautiful form of love. Therefore, love yourself and love others.

Chapter 9: Mistakes and Pain

Can you view your life as making "no mistakes"? I know it sounds absurd to some of you. Thoughts may be running wild in your head at this very moment of all the horrible things you did in the past. I am not surprised—that is your false self in control. Or you may have thoughts such as I should have bought that house, taken that job, married that person, or never married that one, moved to that city, etc. You can probably think of a million things that you label as mistakes. Why do you torment yourself in this way? It's because you are not living a harmonious life at this moment and you try to find a reason from your past instead of working on your present situation. This prolonged type of thinking leads to emotional pain and disharmony. But if you live with a connection to God and connection to self you will know that all things progress toward your highest good. Therefore those actions were not mistakes. They came into your life to teach and bring you to a greater awareness of self. The results of those choices molded you into who you are today. They may not have been pleasant and may have been seemingly bad choices but they were not mistakes. You made them at the time based on your level of consciousness and your sense of self. As you evolve and grow you will reflect on those and discover that those choices were the only ones you thought were available at the time.

When you become self-aware it's as if a whole new platter of life is served to you. It's like discovering that there are many more types of wonderful cheeses in the world instead of only Cheddar or Brie. It's the same as knowing that there is an entire ocean but you can only see a sliver of it through your window. Even though you only see a portion of it, the fact is an expansive body of water exists. When we connect with God and become self-aware an expansive, unlimited set of choices becomes available to us. The belief that your life is filled with lessons and not mistakes will liberate you and lead you on the road to self-discovery.

I know it's hard for many of you to view your life in this fashion because you criticize yourself for everything you have done wrong. This type of thinking will keep you separate from source. For one, it's a trick to keep you living in the past and for another, it wants to sabotage your future. You must remember that you are not "your mistakes or your pain." What you are is an individualized expression of God. Begin to view yourself that way and you will disassociate from your mistakes and pain. You must also know that the "law of circulation" is at work and every time you are meant to learn a lesson it will be presented to you over and over again in different scenarios until you have learned what was necessary from it.

Chapter 10: Intuition

"The intuitive mind is a sacred gift and the rational mind is a faithful servant. We have created a society that honors the servant and has forgotten the gift" - Albert Einstein

Einstein also said this, "The really valuable thing is intuition. The intellect has little to do on the road to discovery. There comes a leap in consciousness, call it intuition or what you will, and the solution comes to you and you don't know how or why."

"The power of intuitive understanding will protect you from harm until the end of your days." ~ Lao Tzu

What is intuition? It is not one of the five senses: touch, taste, smell, sight, or hearing. Instead, it is an inner sense or what I would call a "soul" sense. It's very normal for people to rely on their physical senses but not very much on their inner senses. Why? Because we are not taught to do so. Ingrained in our brains is the use of conscious reasoning or logic. Intuition is the ability to understand something without conscious reasoning. Another way to describe it is to allow a "gut" feeling to take precedence over consciousness. Have you ever had to make a decision about something and you knew without a doubt that you made the right one? You didn't need to spend grueling hours thinking about it or days doing research or using some schematic logic, instead, your "gut" just told you what to do. This is intuition. Or perhaps you prayed about an important decision and asked God to direct you. When the time came to make the decision it was easy to do so. This is intuition. It's a feeling in the heart. Some people know it's their intuition because they can physically feel it inside their bodies. It could be a tingling or warm sensation or a gentle thump in the heart. I like to call it "divine guidance." It is the higher self or wiser self that lives in the present and wants to guide you. For me, trusting my intuition is trusting that God is directing me, therefore I know that all my decisions will be the right ones.

Since you are not taught to do this in the school systems, it is a skill that you must learn how to develop. It is done like any other skill you want to perfect—you practice it. Next time you must make a decision instead of going through all the normal conscious gyrations say a quick prayer and ask your higher power for guidance and then do the next right thing. I used the word, "right" because intuition will never lead to "wrong." Once you begin to do this a few times and see the positive results the process becomes easier. Before you know it, you will be doing this unconsciously because you have built your spiritual muscle to do so. Over time you will notice positive changes in your life and body. The space that once held stress is now being filled with inner peace.

Do you realize that every day you get inundated with information from many sources that flow into your subconscious mind? Much of it can be useful, but I do see a potential problem that it presents to you. The problem arises when the information you are given leads you away from trusting your inner spirit, as opposed to moving you closer towards it. I will give you an example. My friend relayed information to me about Mercury Retrograde after participating in a group discussion. She expressed enthusiasm and mentioned the (do's and don'ts) she was advised to follow during the retrograde period. I realized after listening to her that many people who hear those things live anxiously during that time. They believe they are at risk of bad things happening if they don't succumb to the advice. She also mentioned that everything had gone wrong for her on a particular day because it was a retrograde day. Could that have been the power of suggestion? I am not claiming that certain incidents such as electronic hardware and software breakdowns or other things are not related to retrograde because it is a possibility. But what I am stating is that our human minds are susceptible to the power of suggestion and find it comfortable and easy to give a name or a reason for the unexplainable situations in life.

Here is another example related to Mercury retrograde. Advice is given that you shouldn't make a contractual decision during that time. Let's say you wanted to buy a house and you believed that the house was meant for you. But your friend told you about the retrograde and you said to yourself, "I want the house but I shouldn't sign a contract during this time, I will wait until after the retrograde." This imposed idea has ruled you and moved you away from your divine inner spirit's guidance. Therefore, you have just given your power over to that idea instead of trusting your own intuition. The choice to not sign the contract resulted in you losing the house that should have been yours. If you made the choice from your intuition to not sign it, then losing the house would be for your highest good. But when a choice is made out of fear, it's not for your good. FEAR and GOODNESS are opposing energies and don't work together.

I talked about the power of 3's in the introduction, three is a powerful number and you have heard it said that you must do things three times before you make a decision. This idea has translated into many areas of our lives, especially related to the dating scene. Dating experts say to go on a date three times with the same person before making a decision. It may be good advice if it's your first time dating, but when you are in tune with yourself you will know if you want to go on a second date or not. You don't need to be dictated by the law of three if it moves you away from your true spirit or connection to self. I have heard stories of women who endured three horrible dates just to stick to that rule. Perhaps the reason for their singlehood is the inability to trust their inner spirit.

Psychologists have long-time studied the phenomenon of suggestion and the intriguing relationship between suggestion, cognition, and behavior. Across many studies, research has shown that deliberate suggestion affects performance on learning, memory tasks, which products you prefer, and how you respond to supplements and medicines. This accounts for the well-known placebo effect. Many people become well after taking "fake medicine" because a doctor stated it would improve their health. Couldn't you listen to your own inner spirit to guide you toward good?

Humans always want to find a reason for events that

happen in their life instead of realizing that they are a result of their actions congruent with their thoughts. I find it quite amusing and it proves our human nature once again. Could imposed ideas and some of the information you take into your mind be controlling your choices instead of you letting your intuition be in charge?

When things don't go as planned in your life do you pass it on to another or blame it on something other than yourself? Does this sound like a "lack of responsibility"? Are you always looking for reasons? This will not lead you closer to trusting your intuition. Instead, it's important to understand those things that happen to you are the result of your own thoughts and desires aligning with your spirit.

As I said, some of the information you absorb is useful. But beware; it's easy to give your power over to those imposed suggestions without knowing it. The information is not useful when you no longer trust your intuition. Once you know yourself, you will trust yourself. The lack of a connection to self will result in a lack of inner peace.

Chapter 11: JOY

It's not by chance that this topic is in chapter 11 because the number 11 has guided me in many ways and it gives me joy to give my message of hope and transformation to the world. On my journey, I have discovered that it is important to do things that bring you joy if you want to have inner peace in your life. If you don't know what prompts the emotion of joy it's because you aren't connected with yourself. Do you feel this is you? Are you stressed and haven't allowed yourself the luxury to find what brings you joy? Have you said, "I don't have time now?" or "I will do it later, or next year, five years from now, or when I retire." You must realize there is a problem with that way of thinking; that time may never come for you. Therefore, you must seize the opportunities available to you now. Now is the time for you to begin to do the things that you love. You will never feel a sense of inner peace unless you do. Life is not all about work. You must create a balance between the two. Life is short and it is meant to be lived to the fullest.

Perhaps one of the problems is that you don't believe that you have a right to experience joy. If this is you, begin to change your thoughts and know that it is a God-given right available to you and to everyone. Don't wait until it's too late or a tragedy hits you to find yours, as I did. You are reading this now because you have the opportunity for joyful things to come into your life. So ask yourself, what is it that you would like to be doing? Is it dancing, painting, traveling, or anything else? You are a unique individual and there is something that will bring you joy. If you don't know what it is yet, begin to experiment. Take some classes and try something new. Be adventurous; be creative. You won't know until you try.

Everything in my life changed after Steve died and one of the things I discovered on my journey of recovery was tango. People who are lonely and ridden with pain often find their way to dance and many to the tango for various reasons. One is that tango allows you to be held by another human being. It is not in a sexual way—it is in a sensual way. Dancing tango is a way for someone who is afraid, lonely, or filled with heartache to let go of painful feelings for the moments they are gliding along the dance floor. They think of nothing except the dance. It allows you to feel the warmth and energy of another human being. It's also interesting to note that people often carry their persona in the way they carry their bodies. For example, someone who is in emotional pain or has little self-confidence often stoops over with poor posture. The tango can transform this type of person because an upright position is required to dance the tango well. This new position helps them become a better dancer and can also bring confidence into their life. This newfound confidence creates harmony and balance.

I know that I was divinely guided to it for many reasons. One was that Argentine Tango became my lifesaver. And second, it led me to find love again. I met my husband Gerry because of tango. Dancing tango has been transformative for me and it certainly is a metaphor for life. Today it continues to bring me great joy!

Gerry and I both have the same passion for it and we dance it on a regularly. When we travel to new places our number 1 priority is to dance at a local tango club. Even if we don't know the culture or the language of the places we visit we know that we will have a wonderful connection with others because of the love of tango. Don't wait to find things to do that you love.

Inner peace will never be demonstrated in your life if you continue to cling to unhappiness. It is contrary to the spiritual law of cause and effect, just as no man will remain dry if he jumps into the ocean.

Chapter 12: Identify with Yourself

What it means to identify with yourself is to know what you think about yourself. Do you think you are a good person? Do you think of yourself as a good spouse, parent, daughter, son, or friend? Do you think you are a positive person or are you generally negative? Do you think you are healthy or unhealthy? Are you a drinker? Are you a smoker? Are you a golfer, artist, or writer? These are the questions you must ask yourself to know yourself. Whoever you identify yourself as—you will be or become. For example, if you think of yourself as a smoker, then mostly likely you will be a smoker for the rest of your life. Even if you say you want to stop smoking chances are you won't kick the habit. The reason is that you created an identity about yourself as a smoker. Most people don't succeed at quitting because of their attachment to their identity. Your conscious and subconscious mind knows you as a smoker. So if you want to change it you must see yourself and know yourself as a non-smoker. Also, you must see yourself as someone who doesn't want to be labeled as one. You must begin to look at yourself as an ex-smoker. You may not believe it initially and that is OK. The first step is to begin seeing yourself as a non-smoker and saying it to yourself. You can do this by looking into the mirror each morning and saying, "I am a non-smoker." Also, begin to tell others you are a non-smoker, and when you say it don't smoke in their presence. The belief will come eventually and once the belief is put in place you will be led to the tools that will help you. That's when the magic happens!

The image you create about yourself is what ultimately creates your reality. You unconsciously move in the direction that keeps the images of who you are alive. So if you begin to see an image in your mind of yourself as a non-smoker, then you will move in the direction to become one. Events will occur that lead to your desires and soon your new identity will emerge as a non-smoker. One explanation for not succeeding at your goals or desires could be because you haven't changed the image of yourself and it's ultimately keeping you stuck. Do not forget that your mind is more powerful than any addiction. Life-long habits of wrong thinking can be replaced with right thinking.

Another example is related to body image. If you see yourself as fit and trim you will do things in your life to keep yourself that way. Those who see themselves as fit and trim usually have a regular exercise routine. They act on the belief they have about themselves and the image they have created in their mind. Most likely they have a healthy eating style as well. They may waiver at times, but they know in their mind that they are fit and healthy and want to remain that way. If they jump off the bus at times they get right back on and take the ride to keep them fit. I have just given you the most profound yet simple reason why people are successful and achieve their goals. You can't be successful with a negative identity nor can you have inner peace. Begin to imagine yourself as to how you want to be. Create your new identity with your thoughts.

My former identities dragged me down and served no purpose, but my new thoughts put me on a different path. I now see myself as living with the light of God in and around me that can shine into the world and make a difference. One way I did it was to share my experience of grief in a book I published, "Be Gentle with Me, I'm

Grieving." It was hard to "come out" per-se and talk about my husband's suicide because of the stigma associated with it. But I did it because I listened to my higher power and I am grateful that my book has benefited others. My whole identity changed and I was driven to become a coach so I could help those who grieve or are in a stuck state. I no longer identify myself as a grieving widow, a lost soul, or a victim. Instead, I identify myself as a unique expression of God with unlimited potential that always creates its highest good.

I also identify as a tango dancer. This is a very large and special part of my life. It fills me with passion. It's an expression of who I am. I let myself connect with the music, the dance floor, my partner, and myself. It allows me to live in the present moment, free from any worries, anxieties, or pain. It has profound meaning to me because it was the catalyst to get my life back after Steve's death. I discovered it while on my journey of creating my new identity. The dance breathed life back into me. I feel intense gratitude that I have met another man with whom I could love and share my life. Many people have said to me, "you are so lucky." I don't view it as luck, because it wasn't by chance that I met Gerry. It happened because of several universal laws at work. I knew that I didn't want to spend my future alone. I began to see myself as happy and in love. I had an image of myself in love, just as I was with Steve. Of course, it would be different, but I knew the experience of giving and receiving love was part of who I am. I felt it in my heart. I imagined it and then the reality of what I desired followed.

I also have other things I identify with such as, I am a golfer, a cyclist, a tennis player, a writer, a teacher, and a speaker. It's important for you to find your identity. You can create new ones at any time in your life. Sadly, they are often forced upon you after loss or tragedy. It's during the grieving process that one often searches the soul for answers. Loss strips away your current identities leaving you to create new ones. Roles and identities constantly change throughout life and certainly from loss. Perhaps you were a soccer mom and sadly your child died. You no longer have that role for your deceased child. It's during those difficult times that the search for a new role begins. Perhaps you decide to become a yoga student or enroll in a cooking class. Whatever it is, it's important to identify with something that brings you joy. It is never too late to create any new identity. You will never connect to yourself unless you do. This is a necessary step for creating inner peace.

Exercise:

Write down how you identify yourself. Be honest. Even if

it's negative you must write it down, such as procrastinator, jealous, or controlling person. Remember, you can't change it unless you first become aware of it. Exercise:

Write down how you identify yourself. Be honest. Even if it's negative you must write it down, such as procrastinator, jealous or controlling person. Remember, you can't change it unless you first become aware of it.

1. I identify myself as _____.

2. I identify myself as _____.

3. I identify myself as _____.

4. I identify myself as _____.

5. I identify myself as _____.

Don't limit yourself to these five if you have more.

Now, I want you to list how you want to see yourself, such

as happy, serene, a peacemaker, in a relationship, learning a new skill, etc. Write those down and actually see yourself in your minds eye in that role. Make the image appear on a big screen in front of you in full color so you see it clearly in your mind.

1) I now identify as_____.

2) I now identify as_____.

3) I now identify as_____.

4) I now identify as_____.

5) I now identify as_____.

Your assignment is to see your new identities each morning and night before you go to sleep. Keep the image big and full of color. Also, throughout the day act like you are going to the movies and sitting in front of a big screen, then bring the image to your mind. These exercises will begin to change your brain and your reality will eventually change because form follows thought.

As you move toward inner peace you must begin to see yourself as one with God or source. This must be added to your list but you must go through the exercise of knowing yourself and identifying with yourself before you can identify with source.

Man is created with the possibilities of limitless freedom to discover his true self and true essence. You must know that you have everything necessary within yourself to live your earthly life in a joyful paradise. It is your divine birthright and you must choose to accept it. Hold this thought in mind; there is no scarcity, only abundance. This is the universal law of abundance. The universal laws are always operating if you believe them or not, so why not choose to do so!

130

Chapter 13: Dreams

I have heard many people say they don't dream. You too may say it about yourself. I am not referring to dreaming or fantasizing about things you desire. Although, doing so helps bring them into your life. I am talking about dreaming while sleeping. We all do it. What we don't do is remember them. Research suggests we should sleep between 7-8 hours a night. During some of those hours we go into REM (rapid eye movement) sleep and it is during that time that we dream. Why is this important? Because dreams are a gateway to our subconscious and they lead to more self-discovery. There is much written about the dream world and dream symbols. Dream specialists, books, and workshops can teach you to interpret them. I have been to several workshops and learned to interpret my own. Even though some dreams seem scary and nonsensical, they always have a positive message.

In one of my dreams many years ago someone I knew was drowning. They were hysterically flapping their arms in the vast ocean trying to stay afloat. Of course, the dream caused me to wake up in a cold sweat. You may have had that happen as well. If I didn't understand dreams my first reaction would have been fear and I may have called the person to tell them, never to go into the water again. It sounds outlandish, but dreams often induce fear. But since I had learned how to interpret mine there was no fear. Why did that particular person show up as drowning? Because I had thought about him during the day or something related to him. I can always trace the reason certain people and experiences appear in my dreams. They are based on the thoughts in my waking state throughout the day. Some dream experts believe that every character in your dream is a representation or an aspect of yourself. This holds true for me. My interpretation of this dream was that "I" was drowning. Not physically, but emotionally. The dream gave me insight into what I was doing. I was overcome by guilt from my husband's suicide and the message to me was—if I didn't release the guilt then I would emotionally drown in it. If I hadn't learned about dreams I wouldn't have related it to my current emotional state. It came to me at the right time when I could make the connection with the effect of grief on my life. It caused me to do some inner work and I discovered much of my guilt stemmed from childhood.

I also had many other dreams after Steve died about my car. In each one, someone had stolen it from me. It was apropos in my world since Steve always wanted to be behind the wheel when we were together. I felt my identity was stolen after he died. He was the driver and the one who always led the way. The dream helped me realize it was time to create my new identity and learn to drive on my own. Dreams come from our inner or higher self and they want to reveal something to us that will lead us closer to our true selves. We often don't live in the realm of our true potential and that is why a connection to self is so important. It guides you to discover your divine nature. Dreams are one way to assist you.

If you don't remember your dreams don't worry, there is nothing wrong with you. Here is a method you can do to help you retain them. First, before sleep, tell yourself that you want to remember them. Say out loud, "I want to remember my dreams tonight and I am open to receiving them." This is a command to your subconscious to do so. Second, when you wake up in the morning ask yourself, "what did I dream"? Do this before you allow any other thought to enter your wakeful state; otherwise, the busyness of your mind will instantly push the dream out. Also, keep a notebook and pen near your bed. If you wake during the night, write the dream on paper immediately. Also, keep a journal and write down your dreams anytime you remember them. You may see a pattern in them. These are messages to you from your higher self. If you haven't tried it, go ahead and start. If you can't interpret your dreams I recommend you read Diane Brandon's book, "Dream interpretations for Beginners: Understand the Wisdom of your Sleeping Mind."

Part III: Connection to Souls

The third *must have* connection that is needed to find inner peace is a connection to souls or in other words, a connection with other people. You can't survive in the world very long without making a connection to another human being. If you entertain the idea of creation then the importance of connection to souls makes sense since Eve was created as Adam's companion. It was not good for man to be alone. Nor is it good for you to isolate yourself from other people. Of course, as I discussed in chapter 1, you need your "alone" time, but you need interaction with others as well. Everything in your life must be balanced and operate according to universal laws for inner peace.

Do you ever wonder why you are attracted to certain

people or why certain individuals suddenly show up in your life? Think about the last time you were at a party where you didn't know many people. Did you find yourself gravitating to some and avoiding others? This is because there are two universal laws at work. One is the "law of attraction" and the other is the "law of reflection." These universal laws seem to be life's biggest mysteries, but they are continuously at work. The law of attraction states you attract what you are concentrating on or where you direct your thoughts. Therefore, if you are negative, you will draw into your life an experience of negativity. And the opposite is also true. If you have loving energy then more loving people will enter your realm. Another way to say it is this, "where your attention goes, your energy flows." You will only attract those qualities that you possess.

The universal law of reflection states that the traits you respond to in others are those that you recognize in yourself, both positive and negative. It has four primary manifestations:

1) That which you admire in others, you recognize as existing within yourself.

2) That which you resist and react to strongly in others is sure to be found within yourself.

3) That which you resist and react to in others is something that you are afraid exists within you.

4) That which you resist in yourself, you will dislike in others.

Test the law by thinking in detail about the most recent people you have met. Get a picture of them in your mind and your interaction with them. Think about their character, their actions, the words they use, and how they interact with others if applicable. For example, did you find yourself attracted to someone who had a standoffish attitude or was condescending? Maybe you realized you have those same qualities in your own life and have been resistant to change? Or did you find yourself drawn to someone incredibly bubbly and lighthearted? Does the law hold true when you think about the people in your life? They have come to you for a reason. Look at each one as a messenger to bring awareness to you. Thus, it's the reason to connect with souls. It creates growth in you.

American psychologist Abraham Maslow created the five hierarchy of needs to reach self-actualization and number three is about connection. He defines it as love and belongingness needs which consists of friendship, intimacy, trust, acceptance, and receiving and giving affection and love. You must affiliate yourself in some capacity with family, friends, work, etc. You must make connections in your life. We all need bonding relationships in our lives to keep us healthy. Are you one of those people who think you don't need them? Do you isolate yourself from others? Do you find that you end up destroying your relationships? Could lack of understanding or not trusting your own judgment be the reason for it? You must have a connection with yourself before you can have a genuine connection with another soul. It's necessary to have all three connections that I refer to in this book to attain inner peace. It's a complete package. You can't have one without the other, just as waves cannot be created without a body of water.

Too often, people sabotage their relationships because of unresolved issues carried forth since childhood. Many stem from being abandoned, bullied, or abused. If you are not connecting with others it's important for you to uncover those reasons. Don't believe that any of your faults, bad behaviors, or things from your past must always be a part of you. This is not true. You always have the potential for change.

Problems arise when you are stuck in your attachments from childhood. If you have been deprived, controlled, rejected, and haven't dealt with those feelings they can create havoc in your current relationships. Unresolved issues will affect your own sense of well-being. It's necessary to become aware of them. Connecting to others can help you. How? Relationships are the gateway that will bring out your best and worst qualities. It's the worst that you must become aware of before you can make a change. In the end, you must view what apparently seems like a bad relationship as something that could result in good and something that allows you to learn. This viewpoint will help you move in the direction to create a healthy lifestyle that brings inner peace.

You may be thinking it's just too hard to make connections with others. You may find yourself constantly in the presence of angry, bitter, mean-spirited people. If this is you, then you need to turn and run the other way when you see them coming. But you must realize there is a reason they continue to enter your path. You are attracting the very thing that you don't want in your life. Thank the "law of attraction" for bringing the wake-up call to you. It has presented an opportunity for you to change. Remember, what you habitually think about will eventually come into your life. Like attracts like, therefore, there are qualities that dwell within those people that also reside in you. It's now your time to discover it. If you haven't yet, go back to Part II and do the exercises to connect with self. If you want change to occur, then you must make a change. You cannot expect others to change themselves for you nor expect them to change you. It is you that must do the work.

Awareness of your unpleasant qualities must come from within as well as a desire to change. You cannot place blame on another person for your inability to have meaningful relationships. It's time to take a long look in the mirror. I didn't say that this would be easy. Do you think that attaining inner peace ever is? What in life doesn't come without effort? But in the end, it will help you prosper.

When Steve died by suicide I felt that I was the one to blame. Guilt kept me stuck in the inner chambers of hopelessness. Grieving opened the floodgates to all the pain I had carried as a young girl. My eyes gazed long and hard into my mirror and one day they pierced me with the realization that I had carried guilt since my childhood pregnancy. Through my grief work, I learned the power of forgiveness, which allowed me to release the ball and chain of guilt. No one did it for me. I did it with help from my divine source which gave me the strength to do the inner work. My grief journey brought about my transformation and gave me the gift to discover the three connections for inner peace.

Exercise:

Write down what keeps you stuck in your life. Is it grief? Is it a lack of self-confidence? Is it guilt? Is it shame?

Write it on paper. And then think about the time it started. Spend some time thinking about the event. I am a firm believer in writing things down. The words on paper make it real and allow you to connect with the experience and then do the work. Be honest, it is for your eyes only.

Stuck State	Time in your life	The event that caused it

Now that you have put it on paper, realize that it is in your past. You can't go back and change it, but you can release it. How? One symbolic way to do so is to burn the paper that holds the experience that caused the stuck state. Quiet your mind and ask your higher power to allow you to let the past be the past. Burn the paper with the intention to release those that keep you stuck. Once it is burned to flames it can no longer return to you. Or, if you prefer another method, scribble over your past with a black magic marker. I like the word "magic" and metaphorically there is a magic power in the marker to remove your stuck state from the past since you can no longer see it. Therefore, it has no control of your mind. These exercises are designed to help you realize that your past only has power when you allow it.

The next step after you have released your past is to think of your future. Imagine a similar situation that you just erased will occur two weeks from now. How would you like to handle it? Remember, you have the chance to think about it in a positive way and handle it the way you choose. Write on paper how you will deal with the situation. Let this be your new way of coping with the next event that occurs in your life. You are free and the past no longer has control over you. This exercise can be done with anything that has kept you stuck.

The spiritual "law of giving and receiving" is at work

as you make connections with others. Without it, relationships cannot endure. They are built on the ability to give a part of your essence to another human being and at the same time to receive something in return. It may be the gift of love, caring, doing something kind, or just being available when someone needs you. True, loving relationships are established when you do both, giving and receiving. Are you one of those people who can give freely, but have a hard time receiving? Did you ever think that the reason is because you don't feel you are deserving of it? Many people feel this way, but it is wrong thinking. The person who gives to you does so because they believe you are worthy of it. Do not take this gift away from them. People express their love by giving. It brings them joy. So why do you deny them this right? You must think about this if you want to make true connections with souls.

Do the following exercise to analyze your relationships.

List the five main people in your life and their relationship to you. Then list the gifts or the ways in which you show your appreciation for them. Also, list the things they do for you.

Below is my example. Make your own list and determine if there is a balance between your giving and receiving? This is an evaluation tool and with this knowledge you can begin to make any necessary changes.

Relationship	Person	What you give	What you receive
Husband	Gerry	I give him time to play golf and do all other hobbies without complaining	He makes time to edit my writing whenever I need it
Daughter	Jennifer	The months we live in the same state, I make her a priority	She does the same for me during those months

I am an empath—someone who can sense the energies of others. It allows for making connections easily. Actually, I usually talk to anyone, anytime, anywhere, and usually about anything. It's not rare that while I am standing in a Starbucks line I have an intimate conversation with someone. Usually, others want to tell me very personal things. I exhibit a non-judgmental demeanor therefore people feel safe with me. They often surprise themselves that they have shared openly with me. Those encounters throughout my life validated my desire to help others and become a coach.

I have the ability to determine who is approachable and who isn't which is a characteristic of my intuitive nature. I have a personal story of an interesting meeting that you may find amusing, especially if you are a wine drinker. I consider myself fairly knowledgeable about wine since I have traveled to Spain, Italy, France, Argentina, and

Germany to taste the grape varietals and learn about the climate and growing processes. I also enjoy a delectable, well-prepared meal cooked at home paired with a glass of wine.

A week before Thanksgiving I was shopping in Trader Joe's and there happened to be a wine tasting to pair wines with free-range turkeys. Since I am no longer a wine snob I wouldn't pass up a taste of a $7.99 chardonnay. I began a conversation with a woman who stood next to me. It lasted for 20-30 minutes while we tasted several wines. I learned she was Jewish and studied Kabbalah which I didn't know much about, but was curious. Before I departed she asked about my Thanksgiving plans. I told her my husband and I didn't have any since we had just arrived in Florida for the winter. Amazingly, she invited us to have Thanksgiving dinner with her family and Kabbalah friends. My husband always trusts my judgment and agreed to the offer. We spent a delightful Thanksgiving with Eli and her friends. I am glad that I trusted my intuitive nature. Otherwise, I would have missed a connection to a wonderful soul.

Some people may think that was a crazy way to meet and make a friend, but I don't believe there are any chance meetings. I also view every encounter we have with someone as a "holy encounter." I believe that every one of them is for the edification of one of the parties or both. We may not know it at the time, but often find out later. The point of the story is to be "open" to making new connections with souls. It's important for your growth and self-discovery.

Chapter 14: Like-Minded

People

If you are seeking a deeper connection with God it's important to surround yourself with people who already have a connection to God. It wouldn't make much sense for you to spend all your time with atheists or with people that have completely opposite values than you do, although I believe balance is important in life. It's good to understand others' views and morals because it allows you to hold true to your own, but for your spiritual growth it's a good idea to spend time with people who have an inner peace and source connection. They are those who can teach you and help you gain insight into yourself. These types of people can be found in churches, synagogues, mosques, temples, and various organizations or any other place. Enlightened people exist everywhere. They come in many different sizes, shapes, and colors. You know one when you meet one because a sense of calm radiates from them. You become attracted to their essence and want to spend time with them. Be thankful you are in their presence. I believe they have entered your path so you can learn and be blessed by them. The reason they came to you is because you desire the inner peace that they behold. Nothing is stopping you from getting it and they can help lead you to it.

People who have a spiritual consciousness live their life in a remarkable way. It is one that brings peace and exists without worry and anxiety. They live with a sense of knowing that all is unfolding according to the laws of the universe. In other words, their thoughts manifest the activities in their lives. They understand that certain laws govern the universe and if they live without resistance to them their ultimate potential is realized. These types of people don't need to preach to you their way of life because they live it. You have heard the saying, "Actions speak louder than words." The actions of these people validate they live an authentic life. In a sense, you could say they are actually living what they are preaching or teaching. I consider myself one of these persons. I know that people trust and believe in me because what I teach or write about is what I believe and how I live my life. Any challenges that occur in my life keep me humble and honest so I can live my truth and continue to share my message with others. I am following my path according to divine direction and therefore creating what is meant for my life and for yours. Continue on your path and you too will live with a spiritual consciousness.

Another reason to be in the presence of like-minded people is that it makes you feel "at home" and not judged. One example is related to grief. After Steve's suicide I felt alone and that no one could possibly understand what I was experiencing. Thankfully I found a suicide support group. It was a place I didn't feel judged and felt at ease expressing my emotions. In the absence of that group, I would have felt isolated and alone and perhaps stayed in a stuck emotional state. It's important to be in like-minded groups.

It's important to find our "tribe" so to speak or those people who have similar beliefs. Another example is my experience with the number 1. It holds significant meaning to me as I described earlier. I don't talk about it all the time because I know that some people think it's crazy and don't believe in the power of numbers. I certainly do and that's why I talk about it with an entire community who sees 11:11 as well. Those who study numerology understand the energy and guidance behind the numbers. The main point I make here is for you to surround yourself with others who validate you and with whom you can have a real soul connection. They are the ones who can facilitate your transformation and inner peace.

Chapter 15 Social Media

Our day-to-day relationships are affected by social media therefore it's important to discuss it. I believe it's so important that I wrote a blog about it and want to discuss it further. Social media has actually changed the way we live our lives and how we interact with others. It isn't entirely bad. There are always two sides to every coin and there is potential for everything to have good and bad energy surrounding it. All new ideas or concepts come with risks and benefits. But we don't know the results for many of these until they have been in place for a period of time. It's important to be cognizant of the bad so you can avoid them.

The question is; how has social media affected your life? I will talk about both the positives and the negatives.

I happen to believe that the bad is outweighing the good when it comes to social interaction and here are the reasons. First, the generation that has grown up with it doesn't understand the art of communicating, meaning they don't want to talk face-to-face or even speak to another person on the phone. If you are like me and have lived with and without social media, you have seen its effects. If you have children you understand my frame of reference. Rather than talking to us, they prefer to send a quick text. The other issue is that people spend an excessive amount of time on social media even while they are in the presence of others. Are you one of those people?

Have you ever been out to dinner with someone when they picked up their iPhone to respond to a text message? I have! If that wasn't bad enough they continued to spend the next 5-10 minutes looking at Facebook, Twitter, or email. I believe it's downright rude and shows a lack of respect, but our culture has come to accept this behavior. Or, have you been at a party and noticed that most people are on their iPhones and not engaging with others? They may talk in brief and be in your presence, but are they really listening? Are they present? I think the obsession with social media is creating a lack of social skills resulting in less and less connection with souls. Perhaps it is one explanation for depression and anxiety amongst the young, but not limited to them. Think about it; do you see this happening to your children or to you? If you do, it's time to make some changes now! Don't let social media rob you of the experience of fulfilling soul connections or a lack of inner peace.

In order to build a lasting bond and friendship, it's necessary to listen and get to know the other person. It's a two-way street and is certainly needed for a healthy relationship. Studies about Facebook use have shown that users get depressed or sad looking at others' posts because his or her own life is not optimal. They read and see pictures of all the fun their friends seem to be having while they themselves are not. It instills jealousy and exacerbates the sadness or depression they may already be feeling. Do you find yourself upset if someone doesn't respond to your posts by liking, commenting, or sharing them? Does the lack of their interaction make you feel insignificant in the universe? Does it cause you to feel hurt, sad, or angry? If so, you are putting expectations on your friends through social media. You are the one who suffers because their lack of interest causes you to feel unimportant.

Are you judging yourself by the number of friends you accumulate on Facebook? Are you looking for large numbers to feel good about yourself? How many of those connections are real friends? How many of those people do you really want to spend time with or get to know? You are giving too much power to social media. Do you really believe that all those friends who portray a wonderful life are really living that way? Do they do it just to make everyone believe it? Are they hiding behind Facebook and other social media? Keep in mind that Facebook is not always the true image of reality. It's your interpretation of someone's life. Don't let it cloud your mind about yourself or others. Do not let any form of social media determine your individual happiness.

I will flip the coin and argue that despite the bad or negative aspects of social media there is also good. The answer is to create a balance when using it. This takes a conscious effort because Facebook is likened to a drug. It gets the endorphins flowing and you want more and more. It's as if one needs a "detox program" for it the same way an addict needs a 12-step program. I am not implying that there are no benefits because they certainly exist. One is that it's a way to stay connected to friends and family that you can't see often. But again, don't let Facebook stop you from making an actual call to them. There is value in those calls because you are connecting to them through your words and your voice. When you have conversations with others you can often hear their true emotions emanating from the tone of their voice. Have you ever talked with someone and immediately ascertained that they were sad or excited about something? Of course! Why? Because you hear it in their voice and the energetic vibrations carry over to you. It's hard to recreate that with Facebook. Yes, it's being done in texts with emojis and colors, etc. But is that really the truth? Begin to become aware of how this is affecting your relationships.

I don't mean to make it all bad. Another argument for good is the capacity to grow a business and potentially reach hundreds to millions of people around the world.

That is a large benefit because the possibility is slim without it. Another plus is that access to information is instantaneous. Without it, you would need to go to the libraries or inquire in different ways. There are also many social media applications that can enhance your life, such as mind strengthening games, meditation, hypnosis, etc. I have created my own app called "Think Excellent Thoughts." It's step 5 of my 10-step TET approach that is discussed in my book, "Moving to Excellence, A Pathway to Transformation after Grief." So you see, there is good as well. I want to help create the good and be a participant in it. Do you? You must decide for yourself what your relationship will be with it as the world is creating more of it. In summary, don't let social media cause you to lose your ability to connect with others. Don't let social media control you! Remember, you have the power of choice.

Chapter 16: Forgive Others

Forgiveness is key to any spiritual growth. The words of Jesus are, "Forgive them for they know not what they do." You cannot connect to source, yourself, or other souls unless you learn the art of forgiving. What does it mean to forgive? It means to stop feeling anger or other negative emotions toward someone whom you feel has wronged you in some way. And—stop placing blame on someone for something they did to you. It also means to stop requiring the payment of money that is owed to you. That's a big one for many people. Has someone ever borrowed money from you and said they would pay you back and didn't? How did you handle it? My husband and I had a situation where one of our contractors asked us for money. He explained his dire situation. His wife had left him and he needed money to pay for his kid's college tuition. He asked for 5,000 dollars and said he would pay us back over the next two years. We agreed. Sadly, he only paid back 300 dollars. Initially, my husband and I were upset with him, but we realized he didn't have the means to pay it back and we forgave him for breaking his promise. We could have taken a different path and chosen to take steps to retrieve the money. But we both know we are prosperous and grateful that we have the ability to give. This was a lesson for us to learn the art of forgiving. We also understand the "law of giving." When we give, we will receive. It may not be in the way we think or desire, but we will receive some form of prosperity. It doesn't always mean money.

Perhaps you may have had horrible offenses against you that you haven't forgiven. Now is the time to begin the process. You can never attain inner peace without it. You don't need to like what others have done to you or condone their behavior, but you must let your negative feelings go by forgiving and wishing them well on their journey. If you forgive others you will be forgiven. You can't evolve to a higher emotional level unless you forgive and failure to do so is a violation of the law. There is no getting around it. Do you experience inner peace? If the answer is no, perhaps the reason is that you have someone you need to forgive. Don't delay, do it now. Let the process start for you.

Chapter 17: Share with Others

Sharing a piece of yourself with another human being opens the pathways to relationship building. It's important to share your true self, not the self you desire them to see. Don't fabricate an image of what you want them to see in you, this is deceptive and not authentic. If you do this they will at some time discover your dishonesty. People feel safe when you are authentic and honest. If you are an authentic person you won't have fears about being vulnerable because you understand you are human. Others will not be threatened by you and will feel safe in your presence. When a person encounters your energy they will feel at ease and be able to also share with you.

You have probably heard the saying it takes "two to tango." It's one that is very near and dear to my heart because I am a tango dancer. That saying also applies to relationships. If you want to connect with others it's important that you be open and honest with them. You should be willing to openly share about yourself with someone and also listen to what they want to share with you. I am not implying that you share intimate details about your life at your first encounter with someone, but as the relationship grows it's important. Sharing your innermost feelings with another person gives permits them to do so with theirs. As we share with one another, we metaphorically dance with one another. Relationships take time and work but they can become a beautiful dance and valuable lessons about yourself and each other can be learned.

Chapter 18: Understanding

Energies

We are all made of energy and vibrate at different frequencies and are reactive based upon them. This holds true when we come in contact with people. We are instantly repelled or attracted according to the vibrations we feel. This has probably happened to you without your understanding of the reason. Your vibrational energy is co-mingling with the other persons. Think of a particular time when you felt emotion when around a person, either good or bad. Remember the feeling attached to it. Was it warm or cold?

Did you feel happy, sad, angry, or excited? Recalling them will help you become more aware of energetic vibrations.

It's important to learn to understand your energy when you connect with others. Begin to pay attention to how you feel when you are around certain persons. If you never thought about this before you can do this with a checklist. List five people with whom you spend most of your time. Check the boxes of the emotion or feeling you experience during or after your time with them.

This is not a complete list, there are many more. If you experience one not on the list write it in. This is a way to measure how you are affected by their energy. It's helpful to begin the process of knowing with whom you should spend your time and energy. This is an exercise to help you become self-aware and understand your connections. It's important to have them, but only when they are in your best interest. You don't want to remain in those that are destructive.

If you desire inner peace it's important to experience the emotions and feelings that elevate, not deplete your energy.

Name	Tired	Upset	Angry	Sad	Happy	Inspired	Hopeful	Energized
1.								
2.								
3.								
4.								
5.								

You have reached the end of this book and I am grateful that it has found its way to you. I hope that you explore and experience the three connections for inner peace for yourself. I believe if you practice my suggestions you will attain a new level of living. You will learn to live with a sense of awe and wonder. Remember, you have the power to spread peace into the universe and help change the planet one soul at a time. Let's share and stay connected! If this book has been a blessing to you I would love to hear about it. You can reach me by email at robinlchodak@gmail.com.

Love and Light,
Robin Chodak

Afterword

This book came to be written just like all my other published writings. They have been guided by spirit and this one has been no different. It happened in a mystical way and at the perfect time.

Gerry died on September 28th, 2019, and Covid-19 hit in March of 2020. The weeks seemed to string together with no purpose while I felt the weight of personal and collective grief upon my shoulders. It was a painful time and one day I was feeling very lonely, sad, confused, and asked for guidance on how to move through my emotions. I listened and heard a voice in my head. It's the sweet sound of spirit that I know well and it said, "look for the book you wrote 3 years ago. It will bring you comfort." I obeyed the nudge and searched with anticipation for the document on my computer. To my amazement, I found it easily and incredulously it appeared on my computer as such: Three must have Connections for Inner Peace.doc Sep 28, 2019, at 7:47 PM 250 KB Word document. You may wonder what is unusual about that?

Peace in your life2.docx	Jun 1, 2018 at 3:17 PM
Robin Books	May 27, 2019 at 1:22 PM
test qt audio	Jun 20, 2017 at 4:15 PM
Three must have Connections for Inner Peace.doc	Sep 28, 2019 at 7:47 PM
Unfinished Books	Sep 27, 2019 at 12:58 PM

I knew immediately what had transpired came from beyond because what I saw didn't seem humanly possible. Gerry had died around 4:30 a.m. that same morning. I fell into a state of shock and as the day unfolded many people had gathered in my house. At 7:47 PM I certainly wasn't on my computer editing a book, which I had written 3 years ago!

I knew it was a sign from Gerry. He was telling me that the book needed to be published, especially during Covid-19. People needed to discover inner peace just as I have done.

These signs are what I call the mysteries of life in the nonphysical. I could barely contain myself but I understood the greater forces at work. I proceeded to open and read my book. I sat in awe realizing that it was exactly what I needed and it would be for others as well! I read it cover to cover with no changes since I was satisfied with what I had written three years prior. The thought entered my mind as to why I had never published it. Then the answer came! As soon as I hit the save button on my computer I knew it. It was saved at 3:33 PM on April 6th. Wow! I realized that the number 3 was now a guiding force for me. I was led to write it 3 years prior to prepare me when I needed it. Plus the time 3:33 represents the 3 connections I write about for inner peace.

Interestingly my guiding numbers are 11:11 but since Gerry's death, the number patterns with 3 have entered into my realm. I continue to be open and receptive to the signs and symbols from the nonphysical world, which I believe, will always guide each and every one of us to our highest good. It's up to us to listen!

Continue the journey

If this book touched you, please consider leaving a short review on Amazon. Your words help other readers find comfort and support. You may also find comfort and insight in Robin's Grief and Healing Collection.

Each one explores a different perspective on navigating loss and finding meaning again.

Be Gentle with Me, I'm Grieving
An award-winning book offering compassionate reflections from Robin's personal journey after the suicide of her husband. It reminds readers that grief is a deeply personal process that deserves patience, understanding, and care.

Moving to Excellence: A Pathway to Transformation After Grief
A thoughtful exploration of how grief can eventually lead to growth, strength, and renewed purpose.

Ten Grief Lessons from Golf

A unique and reflective book that reveals what the game of golf can teach us about patience, resilience, and healing after loss.

Loss, Grief and Beyond: The 7th Stage of Grief

An exploration of how grief can evolve beyond traditional stages toward deeper understanding, personal growth, and a connection to the deceased.

ABOUT THE AUTHOR

Robin Chodak is grief coach and an author, who writes to support those navigating loss and searching for meaning after life's most difficult experiences. Her journey into grief work began after the suicide of her second husband in 2005. What began as personal journaling—letters written each night to stay connected and process her emotions became the foundation for a deeper sense of purpose. Through her own healing, Robin discovered a passion for helping others find hope and direction after loss.

Robin is a certified grief, life, and spiritual coach, as well as a certified Master NLP (Neuro-Linguistic Programming) practitioner and Reiki practitioner and meditation teacher. She offers one-on-one coaching and has created an online course for those who desire to become a grief coach.

Her writing has appeared in publications including *The Daily Word*, the *American Foundation for Suicide Prevention, Catholic Charities Loving Outreach to Suicide Survivors*, and *SOSBSA (Survivors of Suicide Bereavement Support Australia)*. She has also contributed to the anthologies in *Tales of Our Lives: Fork in the Road* and in *From Grief to Greatness*. She was also featured in the *Chicago District Golf Digest*.

After finding love again and marrying Dr. Gerald Chodak, Robin experienced another profound loss when he died unexpectedly in their home in 2019. This season of grief deepened her understanding of the grieving process and further inspired her writing and work supporting others.

Robin divides her time between Florida and Michiana. She continues to write, speak, and offer encouragement to those finding their way forward after loss.

Work With Robin

If this book resonated with you and you are navigating grief in your own life, Robin offers additional ways to support your healing journey.

One-on-One Grief Coaching

Robin offers personal coaching for individuals seeking guidance, understanding, and support during grief and life transitions.

Grief Coach Certification Online Program

For those who feel called to help others through loss, Robin has created an online program designed to train and certify compassionate grief coaches.

Other Resources by Robin: Udemy courses

- Be Gentle with Me, I'm Grieving
- Grief, A New Way of Thinking
- Change Your Brain, Create an Excellent Life

To learn more about these opportunities or connect with Robin, visit **www.robinchodak.com**

www.ingramcontent.com/pod-product-compliance
Lightning Source LLC
LaVergne TN
LVHW051119080426
835510LV00018B/2120